PREGNANCY GUIDE FOR DADS

A COMPLETE HANDBOOK FOR MEN BECOMING FIRST-TIME FATHERS

BRAD WELLS

TABLE OF CONTENTS

INTRODUCTION

I remember those months after getting married as the ones with the most vivid dreams I've ever had. Debbie and I had enjoyed our intimate wedding reception. We headed for a brief honeymoon at Niagara Falls, looking forward to what we had planned as our biggest adventure: trying for a baby and starting our family. The idea of becoming a father had impregnated not only my daily thoughts but also my subconscious! And so, every morning, I woke up recalling images of the weirdest dreams:

- I dreamed of caring for a litter of talking kittens; they were all hungry, and their little squeaks made me desperate.
- I was walking hand in hand with Mickey Mouse and other cartoon characters.
- Debbie was stranded on a desert island. I had to reach her by swimming against the current, but the waters kept pushing me farther and farther.
- The baby was already born. Debbie handed her to me, and as I held her, I realized that she was entirely made of glass.

You get the picture, right? And the day Debbie showed me the pregnancy test with those two pink strips, my dreams only got weirder and more vivid. I was thrilled about having a baby with the woman I loved. I was excited about becoming a dad. But also, I was terrified! I felt like I had no clue about what was going on inside her body. Every little symptom had me reaching out to my mother and big sister—this was back in the old days when Google wasn't a thing! I was concerned about her health, about the baby's well-being, about labor, and more than anything, I kept wondering whether I was going to be up to the task. Was I dad material after all? How was I going to provide for my family and be a part of the baby's life at the same time? How could I make sure my wife felt taken care of and understood if I didn't understand the whole pregnancy thing?

To make things even worse, I was reluctant to open up with any of my friends back then. I believed that talking about my fears and worries wasn't manly and that they might think pregnancy is a woman's thing. Fortunately, this isn't likely your case. My older daughter is in her mid-20s; yours is a whole new world!

MILLENNIAL DADS AND THEIR STRUGGLES

Nowadays, more dads than ever before are embracing an active role right from the start: Gender roles have become flexible, and men are encouraged to participate in every step of the journey. According to *Pew Research*, millennial dads spend as much as three times the hours with their children than the previous generation of fathers (Livingston & Parker, 2019). No more old-fashioned pictures of dads waiting in the hospital lobby smoking cigars, thank you! Dads today are present at childbirth, changing diapers, bottle-feeding, providing support to breastfeeding moms, and making conscious decisions about education, parenting styles, discipline, and such.

While all this is good news, it also means you may feel more pressure than fathers of previous generations: You know you have a significant role to embrace, which may cause you worries, fears, and concerns. You may feel unprepared to fit this role, and you don't want to overwhelm your partner with your doubts—she's already going through a lot! You may be coping with stress, anxiety, or even depression. Pregnancy and fatherhood cause a sudden shift in your identity as well as in your relationship.

You know that family comes first in your list of priorities, and nothing is more important to you than your partner's healthy pregnancy and delivery. At the same time, you can't help but worry about financial issues: How will you pay for hospital bills, diapers, daycare, and everything else? How can you make sure you balance work-life responsibilities?

Once your baby is born, you may feel better. At least now you can take the matter into your own hands, right? Well... that's what you think until you discover the impressive amount of time newborns spend breastfeeding! Talk about feeling useless, huh? You may struggle to connect with your baby and find that your partner is a whole new person, and you can't easily communicate with her either. You are going through a lot, but you feel you have to bottle up for the sake of your marriage!

Last but not least, while there's plenty of information available online today, you may find mixed messages and become even more confused. Navigating the healthcare system is not easy, especially when it's your first time. You need support and guidance to overcome your confusion.

WHAT YOU'LL LEARN FROM THIS BOOK

After four healthy pregnancies and five babies—our youngest are twins!—I feel confident as a dad, although there are new challenges as children grow. I've been in your place, and I wrote this book thinking about what I would have loved to read back when I was young, scared, and inexperienced, but eager to learn and become the best possible dad I knew my new family deserved.

In the following chapters, we'll approach what I like to call the CRAFT method: It will enable you to prepare yourself for each step of the amazing pregnancy journey you are about to start or maybe are already walking through.

What does CRAFT stand for? Consider, Recognize, Awareness, Fatherhood, and Time.

- **Consider:** This will give you a glimpse of what it's like to be a parent and help you determine if you're ready.
- **Recognize:** This step helps you recognize the signs of pregnancy.
- **Awareness:** This step is about getting information (explanation and details about pregnancy), advice, and tips you'll need as you expect the new family member.
- **Fatherhood:** Here, you'll find helpful advice and hacks to help you ease into your new role as a dad.
- **Time:** Finally, this step reminds you of the need for self-care and time with your partner as you parent your child.

After reading this book, I hope you'll feel empowered, confident, and ready to enjoy the fantastic journey you and your partner are about to live. I'm not here to tell you how to love your baby. You already have what it takes to be a great dad. Read this book to rejoice in the process! And if you can learn something in the meantime, even better.

Are you feeling excited yet? Then, let's get started!

TAKE TIME TO CONSIDER

A couple I met—let's call them Daniel and Juliet—were enjoying the newlywed life. They have just bought a new car and love driving to places during the weekends. Both were focused on their careers and didn't feel obliged to start a family right away. However, everything changed after being invited to the birthday party of one of Daniel's nephews. People began asking them if they had any children, and every time they said "no," they added the word "yet." After all, babies *were* part of their plan, and suddenly, they felt they couldn't wait to get one! Especially since they spend hours looking at other people's babies at the party.

Babies are cute! Their rosy cheeks, their big bright eyes, their chubby legs... It's Mother Nature's trick to ensure we care for them even if they aren't our own. But no matter how much you love babies, deciding to have one isn't something to take lightly. After all, fatherhood is a lifelong commitment. You and your partner should take time to evaluate whether you are ready for this new chapter in your life and your relationship.

IS IT BABY FEVER OR IS IT TIME?

Being surrounded by all those cute little nephews and nieces in their baby outfits, smelling like lavender and roses, and smiling at the birthday balloons during that party, Daniel and Juliet got baby fever. Perhaps you've heard the term before, but is it actually a thing? "Baby fever" describes the sudden urge or desire to have a baby. More than a real phenomenon, it's a colloquial term used to explain the emotion of wanting a child.

How you experience babies around you may influence whether you get a baby fever or not. Believe me: After a six-hour flight next to a crying baby, you may find yourself more likely to get a vasectomy than having a baby. But don't worry! Baby fever is unrelated to your suitability for being a parent: If you've never experienced baby fever and you find out your partner is pregnant, you can still be a fantastic dad! Maybe you get baby fever only after you meet your actual baby, and that's okay.

Some people put a lot of pressure on others—especially women—based on the supposedly ticking biological clock. A woman in her 30s who still hasn't had children is likely to be asked several times why she doesn't have a baby yet. This question causes more harm than good, so refrain from asking it next time! People have all kinds of reasons for not having children. Maybe their financial situation isn't the best; perhaps they have some unresolved health issues they need to sort out before—it can be as simple as having a wisdom tooth removed or as complex as going through fertility treatment—or maybe they aren't *quite there* yet.

If you and your partner are wondering whether it's time to try for a baby, put aside society's expectations. There's a common myth from the 1970s that says women experience a sudden decline in their fertility cliff after 35. Today, we know this isn't necessarily true, and many factors influence the capacity to carry a healthy pregnancy (such as smoking, previous health conditions, and life habits). Women are having healthy children at age 40 or beyond. Besides, fertility issues aren't necessarily a woman's thing: In one-third of the cases, the problem is with the man (Gouza, 2022). Fortunately, these problems can often be treated.

In a few words, the decision to get pregnant should not be based on what others expect. It's something only you and your partner should decide. Having a baby is a lifelong commitment. Don't let statistics, relatives, or even doctors pressure you. Open, honest conversations with your partner are the best way to tell if the time has come.

A GLIMPSE OF PARENTHOOD

After flying home after the family gathering, Daniel and Juliet start discussing the possibility of trying to get pregnant. They are aware that their lives will be transformed by becoming parents. However, they still need to evaluate the extent of this profound transformation before deciding whether they are ready to try to conceive.

First of all, I suggest you assess your relationship. A baby should never be the glue that holds the two of you together when you're otherwise falling apart! Starting a family should be a shared project when you are comfortable and happy with each other. Although it's the biggest adventure and you will grow stronger than ever, a baby can also shake your foundations. Believe me, some days you will look at each other and want to run far, far away—but if the couple is strong enough, you'll overcome the obstacles anyway.

Before trying to conceive, you should both have a medical check-up. I'm sure you know already that health is a significant issue when it comes to trying to get pregnant, but even if you are adopting, you should also consider your mental health. Postpartum depression is a common condition that can also affect fathers. Make sure you have a strong support system and that you are aware of any signs. We'll further discuss this issue in Chapters 7 and 8.

There are financial considerations to take into account. For a start, a baby significantly impacts a household budget. Supposing you already have proper house accommodations and a car big enough to fit a stroller on the trunk, you'll spend on diapers, baby wipes, formula, doctors, health and life insurance, vaccines, daycare, safety devices, and so on. In the long term, you must evaluate more considerable expenses such as education. You and your partner should decide on issues such as parental leave, savings, and child-care options.

Although poopy diapers may scare you now, they are nothing compared to what lies ahead of your parenting journey! Parental responsibilities are legal obligations that bind you to your children until they are old and mature enough to provide for themselves. It's not enough to keep your kids healthy, fed, and dressed. Your responsibilities only increase as your baby grows up and becomes a child. As a parent, you must be ready to make unpopular decisions and keep your children safe, but at the same time, you must teach them to function independently, hold them accountable, support them emotionally, and make sure they develop values that align with yours.

After some weeks and many long talks, Daniel and Juliet decide they are ready to try. They embrace the many changes having a baby will bring into their lives and face the future with optimism while accepting they still have a few things to figure out. Just like them, you, too, will be profoundly changed by becoming a dad.

Although fatherhood is different for every family, and not every person gets equally involved or experiences it in the same way, here are a few ways your life is likely to change:

- **Your daily routine:** At first, you may feel you have no free time. Your baby will take up all your physical and mental energy, and you may even find that your whole identity is reshaped by becoming a father. You may need to work longer hours to provide for your family, take up new household duties, or probably both! And forget about having drinks with the guys after office; you'll need to rush home to cook dinner—or maybe you will hardly wait to get to bed after those long nights of sleep deprivation.
- **Your brain and hormones:** Although the physical impact of becoming a dad isn't as noticeable as the one women experience, having a baby also changes men's bodies. Unlike what happens in women, who experience changes from the moment of conception, in men, these physical transformations aren't directly related to the biological event of becoming a father but to their level of commitment and how much they participate in caring for their newborn. Researchers discovered men experience higher levels of oxytocin and lower testosterone the more involved they are in childcare. Their brains also transform the areas responsible for empathy, nurturing, and emotional response (LoMonaco, 2022). Those hormonal changes promote a deeper bond between the father and the baby, so they are welcome!
- **Your partner's life:** A woman's life is deeply transformed by the whole process of conceiving, being pregnant, delivering a baby, and possibly breastfeeding for a long time. Her changing body will be the most minor surprise! You may feel you don't recognize your partner as she

becomes emotional and vulnerable, but at the same time, stronger than ever before. Your relationship will go through changes as well. Every aspect, from your sex life to your long-term goals and priorities, is likely to be shaken.

- **Your relationship with others:** When you become a dad, your whole social circle will likely change. Some childless friends may disappear into the mist, but you'll also make new friends in unexpected places, such as the playground or daycare. Your relationship with your parents will be reshaped as they become grandparents. For a while, I believed my mom had forgotten that I existed since she only had eyes for her delightful grandchild!
- **Your baby's life:** You are bringing a new human being onto the planet. It's your decision, not theirs! Therefore, you need to fully embrace your responsibilities regarding their physical, mental, and emotional well-being.

As you can see, having a baby isn't a decision to be taken lightly. I don't mean to scare you. Despite all those changes, in the end, you will feel there's nothing you'd rather have chosen in the world when you hold your baby's hand for the first time.

QUIZ: ARE YOU READY TO BECOME A DAD?

Here's a little questionnaire that may help you and your partner decide whether you are ready to embrace the responsibility of becoming a dad. I invite you to take the quiz together. Write down your answers and check. Some questions may be a bit awkward, but it's always best to find out before the baby is on the way. In any case, it's not supposed to be taken too seriously but to work as a starting point for important conversations and set clear expectations.

- Why do we want to have a baby precisely now? What are we willing to do if pregnancy doesn't happen right away?
- Are we set for medical bills? How will we pay for prenatal studies, labor, hospital stays, and pediatricians?
- How will we divide the housework during pregnancy and after the baby is born? Who will get up at night to feed the baby?
- Do our current jobs offer parental leave? Who is going to take it, and for how long? Who is going to look after the baby afterward?
- How do we picture ourselves as mom or dad? How do we want to parent? What do we like about our upbringing, and what would we like to do differently with our child?
- How will we handle stress and conflict resolution? What are our ideas of discipline?
- How will we make time for the relationship once the baby is born? How will we get personal time? How will we handle self-care?
- Are we going to raise our children in a religion? Which values do we want to pass on?
- How do we picture the future as a family? Which role will grandparents and other extended family members have in our lives?

IT'S NOT ALWAYS EASY AS IT SEEMS

When Juliet and Daniel finally decided they were ready to try, the first thing they did was to stop using contraceptive methods. Much to their surprise, a few months later, there was still no baby! Daniel confessed to me that he felt doubt and frustration: "You spend all of your 20s taking measures not to get a girl pregnant, and all of a sudden, it's all you've ever wanted," he said, "and when it doesn't happen, you wonder if there's something wrong with you!"

Sometimes, pressure and anxiety get in the way of a perfectly healthy couple conceiving a child. While teenagers and young people believe pregnancy just happens—hey, it *can* happen, so by all means, if you don't want to become a father just yet, you should stick to birth control—the reality is that for many couples, it takes longer than expected. About 80% of heterosexual couples conceive after six months of trying, and about 90% within a year. If it hasn't happened to you yet, maybe it's simply because you haven't tried long enough!

Also, keep in mind that for pregnancy to happen, sexual inter-course should be well-timed with ovulation. There are many apps available to track your fertility window and plan your pregnancy —although, yes, it takes away some spontaneity from romance and love-making.

However, if you have unsuccessfully attempted to get pregnant for six months to a year, it's advisable to check with a doctor. Before worrying about medical problems, they'll evaluate specific risk factors that can get in the way of fertility, such as:

- smoking, drinking alcohol, or using recreational drugs
- living with chronic stress or not getting enough sleep
- being significantly over or underweight
- having an underlying medical condition, such as diabetes, a thyroid imbalance, or an undiagnosed sexually transmitted disease (STD)
- having been through cancer treatment in the past
- taking certain prescribed medications

If the couple is younger than 35 and has been unsuccessfully trying to conceive for a year, doctors speak about infertility. It has multiple causes, such as, in women, an obstruction in the fallopian tube, an ovulation disorder, or abnormalities in the uterus such as endometriosis; and in men, sperm disorders such as a low sperm count, low motility, or sperm abnormally shaped. Blocked or swollen veins in the scrotum can cause these problems. Premature ejaculation or erectile dysfunction can also make it difficult to impregnate your partner.

Most infertility causes don't have any symptoms. Therefore, doctors need to perform specific tests to discover why a couple can't conceive. An infertility evaluation consists of several assessments, such as:

- a physical examination
- a detailed review of your medical history
- blood tests to check the thyroid and hormone levels and rule out any possible STD
- imagining exams of the woman's fallopian tubes and uterus
- a semen analysis

Unlike previous generations, now we know infertility isn't a woman's thing. In 20%-30% of cases, it's the male partner who has the fertility problem. In another astounding 40%, both partners have factors. So, forget about the bias about women not being able to get pregnant. Make sure both of your doctors know you are trying to conceive and that you are both tested.

Sometimes, the causes of infertility can be tracked, and other times, it remains unexplained, but almost always, it can be treated. The options depend on the results of the evaluation. For example, if infertility is traced to an underlying medical condition, such as an obstruction in a fallopian tube or a blocked vein in the scrotum, surgery can fix the problem. Other times, fertility might be restored with medication. Advanced treatments include intrauterine insemination (IUI) or in-vitro fertilization (IVF). Each treatment has pros and cons; some are more invasive than others, and each journey through pregnancy or parenthood is unique, so make sure you discuss your options with your doctor.

After their first appointment with the specialist, Daniel and Juliet found out it was normal for many couples not to get pregnant right away. They felt relieved to find out there were so many options available. They scheduled the first tests of their fertility evaluation, but there was no need for any. The following month, they got positive on their home pregnancy test. Their journey had begun!

KEY TAKEAWAYS

We've seen the importance of having long, honest conversations with your partner to assess whether you are ready to try for a baby beyond societal pressures and momentary "baby fever." We've also considered the many ways your life will transform once you become a father. And we've also learned that pregnancy may not happen right away.

The rest of the book discusses the signs and stages of pregnancy and how to prepare and support your partner and newborn before, during, and after pregnancy. Let's start at the beginning of the journey, which is recognizing the signs. We'll discuss this in the following chapter.

RECOGNIZE THE SIGNS

At the beginning of a pregnancy, most women display few to no symptoms, and some of them say that they don't even feel any differently. Suppose this happens to your partner, who is actually carrying a new life inside her body. In that case, you are most likely not to be able to tell what's going on... unless you decide to take an active part and learn everything about the most common signs of pregnancy as well as what's normal and what isn't in this very first stage.

It's more important than you think. Knowing and becoming involved in the pregnancy right from the start is not just a way of supporting your partner. Studies show men's involvement plays a huge role in decreasing maternal morbidity and mortality (Gize et al., 2019), so with your knowledge, you are also protecting the mother of your child. As you carefully go through this chapter, consider how the knowledge you get can be used either for reassuring your partner everything is okay whenever she gets anxious (something completely understandable) or, if necessary, to take her to the emergency room if that's the case.

A QUICK BIOLOGY CLASS

We guys can generally get a woman pregnant at any time. However, the chances of pregnancy depend on several factors of the female body. Let's look at the cycles and learn how they can affect the chances of conceiving a baby. I know, you may have studied this subject before in high school, during sexual education classes. Still, if you were anything like me when I was a teen, you might not have paid enough attention (to be honest, by that time in my life becoming a dad was the least interesting thing about sex!).

What Is a Menstrual Cycle, and How Long Does It Last?

Women get their periods every month. This is the way their body repeatedly prepares for carrying a potential pregnancy. To count the days of the cycle, you start on the first day of bleeding up to the start of the following period. Some women have their period every 25 days, others every 30, and some have irregular cycles—meaning they don't always last the same number of days. The average length is around 28 days, the same as the moon cycle, but regular cycles between 21 and 41 days are also perfectly normal.

Ovulation occurs during the second half of the cycle. This is when the ovary releases an egg which your sperm can then fertilize. Some women don't necessarily ovulate every month despite having their period, which explains why it may take several cycles for a woman to get pregnant even if she's having regular sexual intercourse.

Something worth noticing is that many textbooks will place ovulation during day 14 of the cycle. Although this is true for the average 28-day cycle, it's not what happens in shorter or longer cycles. Ovulation occurs around 10 to 16 days before the next cycle. This means that if your partner gets her period every 34 days, she's likely to ovulate between days 18 and 24, later than what common calendars tell.

Tracking menstrual cycles is always a good idea, particularly when trying to conceive. It will allow you to calculate your fertility window and come in handy when pregnancy finally happens. Doctors calculate an estimated due date by counting from day 1 of the woman's last cycle.

Is Pregnancy Possible at Any Time During the Cycle?

There are no 100% safe sex days when it comes to pregnancy. It is possible—which is why you should *always* use some kind of birth control when you aren't trying to get pregnant— but it's unlikely to happen right before, during, or after the period. Women are fertile when ovulating, so it's important to calculate their particular fertility window according to their cycle. During those days, you have more chances to make a baby.

What About Irregular Menstrual Cycles?

Women who get irregular cycles or who skip monthly periods can have more difficulties getting pregnant since it isn't as easy to calculate their fertility windows. This may happen due to extreme weight gain or loss, stress, over-exercising, or some medical conditions we have already explored in Chapter 1. If your partner doesn't always get her period, or if you've been trying to conceive for a year without success, she should talk to her doctor.

However, it's worth noticing that many women with irregular periods will still be able to conceive. To maximize your chances of success, it's crucial to adopt a healthy lifestyle with a balanced diet, no alcohol or cigarettes, regular exercise, and plenty of rest.

Will Contraception Affect the Cycle?

Some birth control methods affect a woman's cycle, and you should take this into account if you want to have a baby. Of course, barrier methods such as the condom, sponge, diaphragm, or spermicide have no influence whatsoever on what happens with a woman's ovaries and eggs. On the other hand, if a woman is on the pill or takes contraceptive injections, her body needs a little adjustment period before "getting back on track" and returning to regular, fertile cycles.

How Long Does It Take to Get Pregnant After Stopping the Pill?

A woman who takes the pill gets monthly period-type bleeding, but she doesn't ovulate. While a pregnancy can happen right after coming off the pill, the best thing to do is to give the woman's body three months of adjustment before trying for a baby. This will allow her to get back to her natural periods. After this time, you may find out her cycles aren't as regular as expected—they are when a woman takes the pill—so if, after those three months, she's still irregular, it may be advisable to check with a doctor before trying.

Is Bleeding Normal When Pregnant?

Periods typically stop when pregnancy occurs. However, it's possible to experience some very light, painless bleeding (more of a spotting) called implantation bleeding, which takes place when a developing embryo plants itself in the wall of your partner's womb. Unlike real periods, this bleeding is usually pinkish or brown, not heavily red.

Some women bleed lightly before week 12 of their pregnancy. While most of the time it isn't anything serious, it's advisable to get her checked by her doctor, midwife, or early pregnancy unit just in case.

KNOW THE SIGNS

When my friends Daniel and Juliet finally relaxed about their infertility scare, it took little time for Juliet to get pregnant. As usual, she was looking forward to the most obvious sign: a missed period. However, even before that, she had the intuition something was going on. For a start, she was more tired and sleepy than usual, and getting out of bed in the morning took her forever.

Also, she suddenly found the smell of fresh coffee strangely repulsive—something she later realized was a common pregnancy-induced food aversion caused by the increased levels of the hormone estrogen.

Let's dig deeper into recognizing the early signs and symptoms before being sure about the pregnancy.

Early Symptoms

As in the story I told you, some women experience early signs and symptoms of pregnancy even when it's too early for a home test to confirm it. Keep in mind that none of these signs is a confirmation of pregnancy *per se*. However, if you are actively trying for a baby and your partner is experiencing some of them, chances are in your favor.

Skipping the Period

Bleeding is the way a woman's body gets rid of the thickening of the uterus lining that occurs every month as the body prepares for a possible pregnancy. When the egg doesn't get fertilized, the uterus sheds that lining, and it comes out of the body in the form of vaginal bleeding. But if fertilization occurs, the lining stays put, and the woman doesn't get her normal flow.

While a delayed or missed period is the most common early sign, it doesn't necessarily indicate pregnancy. We've seen some women have irregular periods, or they can skip them for multiple reasons other than pregnancy.

Food... or Not!

Just like Juliet experienced a sudden dislike for coffee, common food aversions include milk, tea, eggs, meat, onions, garlic, and spicy foods. Additionally, you've probably heard about "morning sickness," although it can happen at any time of the day. At the beginning of a pregnancy, hormonal changes can cause a woman to feel nauseous, vomit, or find specific smells or foods disgusting. Sometimes, they taste something metallic in their mouth even when they aren't eating anything. If your partner has food aversions or nausea, it's better to stay on the safe side and stick to bland foods such as chicken breast or crackers.

On the other hand, some women experience specific cravings during their pregnancy, a sudden desire for a particular item of food that they may or may not have liked before getting pregnant (my wife developed a passion for mushrooms!). In some cases, women crave non-food items, an eating disorder known as pica. Some women, during their pregnancy, feel the urge to feast on ice, soap, baby powder, or earth. Of course, unlike a normal food craving, you shouldn't indulge in pica when the item is potentially dangerous, and it's advisable to talk to your doctor about it, as it may point to a nutritional deficiency.

Changes in the Breasts

When a woman gets pregnant, her body experiences a sudden increase in hormones such as estrogen and progesterone, which are meant to support her developing baby. This may cause breast tenderness, swelling, or tingling even before the missing period tells the pregnancy.

Your partner's nipples also change. They may become sore, and the areolas (the areas around them) look darker. Although this usually happens gradually during pregnancy, some women can tell these signs early on.

Changes in Bathroom Breaks

After confirming the pregnancy, Juliet realized that for the past couple of days, she had been taking more frequent trips to the bathroom at work. Frequent urination happens because the amount of blood in the body increases during pregnancy, so the kidneys must work harder to filter it all.

On the other hand, many pregnant women experience bloating or constipation. If they appear as early as in the first trimester, these symptoms will likely last throughout the pregnancy.

Other Common Signs

Many women experience some of the following early pregnancy symptoms. Although isolated, none of them are indicators of pregnancy; if they happen all together or if you are actively trying to get pregnant, they may be noticeable before reading the result on the pregnancy test:

- headaches
- mood swings
- dizziness
- nasal congestion
- fatigue
- lower abdominal pain
- higher basal body temperature

Confirming the Pregnancy

Since she and Daniel were actively trying to get pregnant, Juliet decided to take a pregnancy test even a few days before her bleeding was supposed to happen. It came out negative! Eventually, as days passed and Juliet still didn't get her period, she took a second test. She carefully read the instructions, which stated to wait at least two minutes before interpreting the result and taking the test with the first urine in the morning (something she hadn't done the first time, as she admitted she was too anxious). This time, the results were clear: A baby was on the way! Let's learn more about these types of tests and their accuracy.

Pregnancy tests work by detecting the presence of the hormone human chorionic gonadotropin (HCG). This hormone is produced by the placenta, something only pregnant women have. Tests can detect HGC either in urine or blood. Home pregnancy tests are basically little plastic sticks with a piece of reactive paper where the woman pees. You can buy them at any store without a prescription.

How do you read the results of a home pregnancy test? It depends on the brand of the test, but what you need to remember is that "positive" means pregnancy, and "negative" means no pregnancy. Some tests display two vertical lines for a positive, a plus sign, or even the word "pregnant." In any case, make sure you and your partner read the instructions that come with the test.

Home tests are easy to take and interpret, but are they accurate? When taken correctly, they offer a 99% accuracy. So, what happened to Juliet? Taking a home pregnancy test too early can cause a false negative when the traces of the hormone are yet too subtle to be detected, and some home tests are more sensitive than others. That's why it's advisable to wait at least until the first day of your partner's missing period to take one, and ideally a whole week. Other tips for better accuracy are using the first urine in the morning and not drinking excessive fluids, as they may affect the results.

Is there a way to get a false positive on a home test? Usually, when this happens, it's because the woman was pregnant then but lost the pregnancy shortly after the egg attached to the uterus wall. Additionally, some fertility drugs can cause a false positive on home pregnancy tests (Cleveland Clinic, 2022a).

The blood tests are even more accurate than the pee tests, but your partner can't take them home, and they are more expensive. You can take her to the healthcare provider to have her blood tested. This is usually done to confirm the results of a test taken at home or when a couple is going through fertility treatment and needs to know the results sooner than with a home pregnancy test. Blood tests are more accurate in the way they not only detect the presence of HCG but also its amount, which can help the doctor determine how advanced the pregnancy is.

POSSIBLE COMPLICATIONS

After getting a positive result on the test, your partner should start taking prenatal vitamins (if she isn't already) and quit drinking alcohol and smoking right away. It's particularly important to take folic acid—in supplements or her diet—to prevent neural tube defects in the developing baby. The pregnant woman also needs to schedule an appointment with her doctor, but there's no rush, as she doesn't need any medical studies during the first few weeks. However, certain symptoms may indicate something is wrong. Notice them and look for medical attention right away if they happen:

- **Bleeding:** It can be a sign of a miscarriage. Although some spotting is normal during the first weeks, you should consult your physician to see that nothing serious is going on.
- **Severe vomiting:** This is also known as hyperemesis gravidarum. If your partner experiences more than the occasional nausea, a doctor should treat her to prevent dehydration or malnutrition that could put both her and the baby in danger.
- **Pain:** While mild discomfort is expected, a sudden lower abdominal pain on a side may indicate an ectopic pregnancy, in which implantation occurs on the fallopian tube and can't go on. It must be treated as an emergency.
- **Miscarriage:** This is the loss of a pregnancy within the first half of it. It happens to 10%–20% of pregnancies, and 4 out of 5 miscarriages happen during the first trimester (Cleveland Clinic, 2022b).

Note that the first trimester is critical for the baby's development. Pregnancies at this stage may end in miscarriage, sometimes without the woman even noticing she was pregnant in the first place. This doesn't mean there's something wrong with your partner or that she can't successfully get pregnant and deliver a healthy baby in the following attempt.

KEY TAKEAWAYS

We've learned how to calculate a woman's fertility window from her menstrual cycle to maximize the chances of pregnancy. We've also learned about which symptoms are typical during the first stages of pregnancy and which others require immediate medical attention. In the following chapter, we'll get more details about what happens to your partner and future baby during the first trimester.

THE FIRST TRIMESTER

After receiving the confirmation of their pregnancy from Juliet's doctor, my friends were ecstatic: Their dream had come true, and they were going to have a baby! As days went by, Juliet wondered if it was normal to feel that... normal! Her initial symptoms had faded, she was still not showing, and although she was obviously missing her period, she couldn't help but wonder if everything was going okay. As weeks passed, some symptoms kicked in, and although they weren't pleasant, Juliet took them as a sign that the pregnancy was right on track.

At the same time, Daniel was overwhelmed with many questions: Would the stroller fit in the car's trunk? What was the best route to the hospital? By the way, did Juliet intend to have the baby in a hospital or at home? What was the best way to share the news with friends and family? How do you change a diaper? Fortunately, he and Juliet still had several months to prepare themselves.

If you are going through this stage of your partner's pregnancy, you are probably feeling equally confused. Don't worry! You aren't the only dad who feels unprepared. After all, a pregnancy lasts 40 weeks (around 9 months). You have time to educate yourself before you deal with an actual newborn. In this chapter, we will discover what happens to your partner and baby during the first trimester, what you should be aware of, and what you should do to support her.

WHAT HAPPENS IN...

Although most people speak about a pregnancy in "months," specialists prefer to approach it week by week, since the changes are so fast and spectacular. Let's see what's going on during this first crucial stage.

Weeks 1 to 4

The pregnancy journey begins when your partner isn't really pregnant. Can you believe it? This is because it's almost impossible for doctors to track down the moment when the actual conception took place. Ovulation dates are always estimated. Plus, the egg can wait around 24 hours to be fertilized by your sperm. So, if you had a romantic Valentine's night and she gets pregnant, that doesn't necessarily mean the baby was conceived on February 14th. To make things simpler, doctors refer to the day your partner had her last period as day 1 of pregnancy.

During weeks 1 and 2, there's no baby yet. Your partner's body is preparing for ovulation by thickening the uterus lining. She can already do some stuff to maximize your chances of success by taking folic acid, having a complete health check-up, and cutting down on cigarettes and alcohol. On the other hand, you can help make a baby by keeping your testicles cool. Instead of an electric blanket, snuggle with your partner. Turn off the heat and keep your laptop away from your lap! Heat slows down sperm production (Donaldson-Evans, 2023a).

Everything changes at some point in week 3. What could have been another menstrual cycle becomes officially a pregnancy when the sperm fertilizes the egg. What begins as a single, unique cell (called the zygote) starts its journey down the fallopian tube. In the meantime, it divides many times, creating a whole cluster of cells —about a hundred in just a couple of days! Your baby is on the way, although neither you nor your partner know it yet.

As the zygote becomes a blastocyst, cells divide into two groups: One develops into an embryo and the other into the placenta. Although you won't find out until the second trimester, your potential baby already has its own set of DNA, which means it's already either a boy or a girl, has encrypted the color of its future eyes and hair, and many other physical traits. In the meantime, it still looks like a microscopic ball of cells.

By week 4, the blastocyst reaches its destination, the uterine wall, where it implants, ready to develop and grow during the following 8 months. By the end of this week, your future baby will be as big as a poppy seed. During this time, around the embryo (what you'll call your future baby for the following weeks), a bag of water (called the amniotic sac) protects it while inside. The cells that will form the body begin to specialize. Some will create the digestive system; others, the heart; others, the hair and skin; and so on.

During these weeks, some women experience the first signs of pregnancy we discussed in Chapter 2, while others remain clueless. After all, they can feel cramps similar to those from their period or even spot their underwear with implantation bleeding. In any case, their bodies are beginning a massive transformation. Within 6 to 12 days after conception, the egg starts to release

HGC, which means the traces of the hormone will soon be notice-able with a pregnancy test.

Weeks 5 to 9

During the second month of pregnancy, crucial changes occur in the embryo. At week 5, the placenta—an organ that connects the future baby to the uterine wall and provides your child-to-be with oxygen and nutrients—is beginning to develop. The mass of cells begins to take shape. Structures like the neural tube (week 5), a pulsing heart (week 6), and tiny buds, which will become arms and legs, take shape at this early stage. Although still tiny, it grows a lot. In week 5, it's like an orange seed, but by week 8, it will already be as big as a rasp-berry, and doctors will be able to spot it on an ultrasound (and if you are expecting twins, you'll be shocked to see not one sac but two!).

During these weeks, if you could see the embryo, you may notice that it looks like a tadpole with a tail that will eventually become its coccyx or tailbone. However, within weeks, you'll be able to recognize structures such as the eyes, ears, mouth, and other traits that resemble more of a baby's. By week 9, health providers no longer speak of your future baby as an embryo but as a fetus, with most of their major structures already formed and some sponta-neous movement starting to occur (although, no, your partner can't feel any kicks yet!). It's time for rapid growth and development.

The hormonal torrent (mainly estrogen and progesterone) is responsible for your partner getting many annoying pregnancy symptoms during this first trimester—from nausea to dizziness, fatigue, swollen breasts, food aversion, and an increased sense of smell. She won't be "showing" yet, and some women even lose weight if they get morning sickness, but she will most likely start to feel pregnant.

Weeks 10 to 13

By the time you enter week 10 of the pregnancy, you are in the third month. Your baby is growing fast! By week 11, tiny toes and fingers separate from the hands and feet. By week 12, its digestive system begins to move into its abdomen. From the size of a prune to being as big as a lemon by week 13, the fetus already resembles a human baby... or a baby-ish alien, to be more accurate. Tiny teeth develop inside its gums, bones, and cartilage shape knees, ankles, and elbows, and its head takes up about half its size.

By the end of the first trimester, your partner's body has likely adjusted to all the hormonal rush, and her symptoms begin to decrease. By week 13, she's probably feeling a little bit more like herself, with fewer episodes of morning sickness, fatigue, and frequent need to pee, giving her a break. Some women start to show a little baby bump, which is actually her growing uterus.

Mother's Physical and Emotional Changes

As we have seen, the first trimester is a physical roller coaster for your partner. Although pregnancy is still invisible to others, many changes take place inside her body. This stage is commonly known for its discomfort: nausea, fatigue, painfully swollen breasts, an increment in vaginal discharge, dizziness... No wonder your partner has a low sex drive, right?

Plus, knowing that she'll become a mother causes different emotions. Sure, she'll feel as happy as you since you were both trying to get pregnant. It's also normal for her to be scared. Just like you, your partner wonders whether she'll be a good mom for the baby to come, but she's also afraid of her physical changes and delivery day approaching (although it's still far away). The first trimester is also a time of uncertainty. The risk of miscarriage is real, and there's also doubt about whether the baby is healthy. Luckily, medical tests will provide comforting answers to help you both navigate the following months more easily.

Should you share the news with friends and family? The answer is entirely up to the two of you. Some couples decide to wait until the second trimester when the chances of miscarriage significantly decrease. But if you want to tell people, that's okay as well. Just make sure you are both on the same page when it comes to talking about the pregnancy.

WHAT YOU SHOULD KNOW...

Having a healthy pregnancy isn't only your partner's job. The more you take an active part of it, the better your chances of having a healthy baby within 9 months. Booking appointments and going to them together is also an excellent way for you to begin embracing your new role as a father and feeling empowered in it. Here's all you need to know about health professionals, medical tests, and prenatal appointments and how to accommodate your lifestyle to better suit your partner's needs during the first trimester of pregnancy.

Your Doctor

When it comes to pregnancy, there's no single type of doctor who can walk the journey with you, but your partner can make different choices. Be sure to explore different options for health providers and evaluate what's most important for you, depending on your particular needs and what your health insurance covers.

Obstetrician-Gynecologist (OB-GYN)

Commonly known as ob-gyns, obstetricians are medical doctors who specialize in women's health and pregnancy. After medical school, they receive a four-year residency program where they learn everything about reproduction, female health, pregnancy, and birth. Some of them specialize in high-risk pregnancies. This should be the best way to go if your partner has a preexisting medical condition, is expecting twins, or needs to have a cesarean delivery (C-section).

Certified Nurse Midwives

CNMs are professional nurses who receive training and are licensed specifically in obstetric and newborn care. Some women with low-risk pregnancies prefer to work alongside them because CNMs provide a much more family-centered approach and opt for birth plans as naturally as possible. They work alongside the ob-gyn, who can assist if complications occur at any point during pregnancy or delivery.

Family Practitioner

These doctors are trained to treat all sorts of health conditions of every family member, and some assist women during pregnancy and delivery. Your partner can have a family practitioner as the principal healthcare provider as long as they don't refer her to an ob-gyn—which they will do if there are complications during any stage of the pregnancy. One good thing about choosing a family doctor is that they can also care for your baby's health once they are born.

Perinatologist

If right from the start your pregnancy is considered high-risk, you may opt for a maternal-fetal medicine specialist known as a perinatologist. They may be the right choice if your partner is over 35, has diabetes, hypertension, a genetic disorder, or has had problems with a previous pregnancy. They are also the specialists you go to when you need to treat fertility problems.

Once you have asked for references from your friends and family and checked with your health insurance, you will probably have a narrowed list of providers. It's advisable to have interviews with several of them and trust your gut. The person who takes care of your partner during the pregnancy and delivers your baby should be someone you're comfortable with and who provides answers to all your questions and concerns.

Prenatal Appointments

You know your partner will need regular checkups with the health provider to ensure she goes through a healthy pregnancy and delivery. But you may be wondering what happens during those prenatal appointments. How often is she supposed to go? What can you expect from them?

The first prenatal appointment is the one that usually takes longer since the doctor or midwife not only performs a physical check-up—which includes taking blood and testing urine—but mostly talks to your partner and you about both your medical histories. The doctor checks your partner's weight, pulse, breathing, and blood pressure to make sure her health is in optimum condition or to treat whatever health issue they may find. During this first visit, the doctor will indicate prenatal vitamins if she's not taking them and suggest some vaccines according to the ones your partner may or may not have.

In the following checkups, the doctor will measure your partner's belly, feel it to check the position of the fetus, indicate any tests or studies required, and answer any questions you may have.

Couples usually look forward to these prenatal appointments because they are the way to know everything's going great with their baby. They get to listen to their heartbeat and learn about their growth. These appointments are the best moment to ask your health provider questions regarding pregnancy symptoms, changes in the woman's body, and how to prepare for delivery day. Make sure to ask the doctor about facilities in which they have admitting privileges so you can start taking tours.

How often does your partner need to get checked? This depends on two factors: the stage of her pregnancy and whether it's low-risk or high-risk. Any healthy pregnancy usually follows this schedule: one monthly prenatal visit until week 28, a visit every two weeks from week 28 to 36, and a weekly appointment for the last weeks of pregnancy (Kam, 2023). However, your doctor may suggest more frequent checkups if your partner is pregnant with twins or if they detect any risk factor before or during the pregnancy. Following up on the prenatal visit schedule is the best way to prevent complications ahead, such as preterm labor or delivery of a baby with low weight, so no matter how busy you both are, make sure you prioritize these checkups.

Tests and What They Do

During the first trimester, doctors suggest some tests to check on your partner and the baby. Your health provider may suggest more tests according to your partner's age, medical history, and whether she had complications during another pregnancy or delivered a baby with congenital disabilities. However, these tests aren't mandatory. You should decide as a couple if you have them done.

Your partner goes through a Pap smear and a pelvic exam to check the health of her cervical cells and detect any possible STD. She also has her blood tested to identify her blood type and Rh (rhesus) factor, detect possible anemia, find out she has immunity to rubella (German measles), and cross out other STDs. According to your specific racial, ethnic, and family background, some genetic counseling can also be suggested. Additionally, a urine test helps her health provider detect a possible kidney infection or diabetes and spot traces of protein that may indicate preeclampsia. This common pregnancy-induced disease should be checked, particularly after 20 weeks of pregnancy.

The first trimester is also when doctors suggest genetic screenings. This is a way a couple can find out their chances of delivering a baby with a chromosomal abnormality such as Down Syndrome or a congenital disability. However, it's worth noticing that most of these tests don't provide 100% accuracy. According to the results, doctors may indicate further exams that are more invasive and aren't risk-free. With your partner, deciding whether you want them done or waiting until after delivery would be best. You must discuss all of your choices with your health provider.

First-trimester screening: This is a non-invasive test, meaning it doesn't involve risks to the developing fetus. It consists of a blood exam of the pregnant woman that measures two proteins and an ultrasound between weeks 11 and 14 that checks the skin behind the fetus' neck (called nuchal translucency). Afterward, doctors cross the results and come up with a statistic of the fetus having any abnormality. If the chances are low, you usually continue the pregnancy without further genetic tests. However, if doctors find any abnormality, they may suggest further studies.

Non-invasive prenatal testing (NIPT): This cell-free fetal DNA test tracks fetal DNA in a blood sample from the mother. It's non-invasive, and its accuracy for detecting Down syndrome and other chromosomal abnormalities is up to 99% (Johnson, 2023).

Chorionic villus sampling (CVS): A CVS is the most accurate test you can get during the first trimester. Doctors don't necessarily recommend it because it's an invasive procedure consisting of getting a tissue sample from the placenta with a tiny catheter through your partner's cervix or a needle through her abdomen and carries a 1% risk of subsequent miscarriage. However, it may be advisable to have it done in specific cases, such as when you have a family history of specific diseases or if you get a positive result on previous non-invasive tests.

Diet and Lifestyle

A pregnant woman is feeding herself and developing her baby. That's why, during these months, it's more important than ever for your partner to follow a balanced diet. However, eating for two may be particularly challenging because of the first-trimester symptoms such as nausea, vomiting, food aversions, and fatigue. Fortunately, the baby is still too tiny to need extra food. Your partner can ensure she gets enough calories and nutrients by eating small amounts of food several times a day.

How can you help your partner fight nausea and food aversions? Offer her cold or room-temperature foods, which are generally better tolerated than hot servings. Liquids and soft-textured meals are also easier to pass. She should avoid spicy food if she suffers from heartburn. Additionally, drinking plenty of water during the day is the best way to ensure she stays hydrated. If she's not feeling particularly hungry, make sure whatever little food she gets is top quality and loaded with plenty of nutrients. During the first trimester, these are the most important:

- **Folic acid:** It's vital for preventing neural tube defects. Besides her prenatal vitamins, she gets folic acid from green leafy vegetables, cauliflower, beets, fruits (particularly oranges and strawberries), beans, nuts, and fortified cereals.
- **Protein:** It's necessary for building tissue. Offer her eggs, lean meat, chicken, and Greek yogurt.
- **Calcium:** It's vital for your baby's teeth and bones, and if your partner doesn't get the recommended daily 1,000 milligrams, she may lose it from her bones and have problems in the future. Ensure she eats three servings of dairy and plenty of leafy greens. Additionally, the doctor may recommend a supplement.
- **Iron:** It's vital for your partner's blood, and she can't satisfy her needs with food alone, so doctors usually recommend a supplement. In the meantime, it can be found in beef, chicken, tofu, eggs, and spinach. Whenever she takes her iron supplement, make sure she combines it with vitamin C for better absorption (pour her a glass of fresh-squeezed orange juice).
- **Potassium:** It's excellent for maintaining a proper fluid balance and preventing high blood pressure. Your partner gets it from foods like bananas, apricots, and avocados.

Now that you know which foods are best to include in your grocery list, let's see which foods pregnant women *shouldn't* eat. Raw and undercooked meat, fish, and eggs can lead to food poisoning and serious diseases such as listeriosis, salmonella, or toxoplasmosis. "These conditions can cause serious, life-threatening illnesses that could lead to severe congenital disabilities and even miscarriage" (Holland, 2023). The same applies to deli meat and unpasteurized dairy: No soft cheese, sushi, soft-served ice cream, or Peruvian ceviche for your partner! Every fruit and vegetable she eats must be washed carefully. Of course, she should also stay away from any kind of alcohol and limit her coffee intake to one or two cups.

Besides eating a healthy diet, the list of pregnancy recommendations includes exercising—following the routine if she already does or asking the doctor for a new workout plan— getting lots of sleep, and including a multivitamin even if she eats all her meals. Yoga routines are perfect for relaxing, and they provide light exercise, perfect for pregnant women. What about sex during the first trimester? With all the hormonal discomfort, some women experience a lull in their sex drive. However, as long as there isn't a complication, sex is allowed during pregnancy, and it's perfectly safe for your baby until the moment the water breaks (Holland, 2023).

WHAT YOU CAN DO...

During this first trimester, the best way to take care of your unborn baby is to be there for your partner. We've seen the mix of symptoms she might be experiencing! Let's see how you can better help her:

Support Your Partner

Going with your partner to prenatal appointments and helping her follow a healthy diet and lifestyle aren't the only contributions you can make. You can also help her in these ways:

- **Quit smoking:** You're not the one carrying the baby, but second-hand smoking is nonetheless bad for pregnancy. Besides, if your partner needs to quit the habit herself, this is the best way to support her.

- **Let her sleep late:** She's experiencing fatigue and sleepiness. Let her rest an extra hour whenever possible. You can make breakfast before she gets out of bed.
- **Lift the heavy things:** Making efforts can hurt your partner's back. Make sure you do all the heavy lifting.
- **Take extra household duties:** Even if you divide the housework equally, allow her to rest. Additionally, being in charge of the cooking can save her from feeling disgusted by specific foods and smells.
- **Stay calm:** While your partner experiences symptoms and mood swings, remember they are normal and temporary.
- **Provide a listening ear:** Let your partner open up about her doubts and fears. You probably have yours, but you should talk about them with a friend with kids, your parents, or a counselor. Don't overwhelm her with more worries.

Prepare for the Next Few Weeks, Months, and Years

Another way to relieve some of your partner's burden is to be in charge of financial planning for pregnancy and after-baby. Having a child costs a lot of money! A 2017 report from the U.S. Department of Agriculture (USDA) states that the average family in the United States spends almost $300,000 raising a kid from birth to age 18—which doesn't include college tuition or accommodation (Batcha & Srinivasan, 2023).

You can tackle as many of the following as early as in the first trimester:

- Sign up for health insurance, both for your partner and the future baby. You should also consider investing in life insurance.

- If you already have insurance, update your beneficiaries to include your partner and future child.
- Check out the cost of prenatal services. If necessary, switch to a better plan as soon as possible.
- Find out about your workplace's parental leave policy.
- Look into special programs and apply if you need financial aid.
- Cut down on your credit card debt.
- Track your current spending and create a savings plan.
- Start coming out with a baby budget. Some ways to save are borrowing maternity clothes and buying second-hand baby gear.

KEY TAKEAWAYS

We've seen why the first trimester is usually the most challenging. The risks of the pregnancy at this stage are at their peak; everything is new, and your partner goes through a lot of discomfort. However, there's plenty you can do to support her. Fortunately, as weeks pass, most women feel relief from their symptoms. The second trimester is, for many, the best part of the pregnancy. Let's look at that in the following chapter.

THE SECOND TRIMESTER

After Daniel and Juliet's pregnancy reached the milestone of 14 weeks, and they were given the good news that their first-trimester screen was normal, they finally decided to share the news with their friends and family. I was among the guests at a fun dinner party they hosted. My friends suggested playing charades, but after a few minutes of them being silly together and laughing out loud, we all found out they were trying to convey a message: "Juliet is chubby," "Daniel is holding a watermelon!" we shouted, although we had pretty much figured it out. After they confirmed the news and showed us a picture of the sonogram, we clapped and cheered, and the party became even happier!

For Juliet and Daniel, and many other expecting couples, sharing the news brings significant improvement, as they get all sorts of social support for the rest of the pregnancy. Juliet's mom and sisters created a WhatsApp group to share tips, healthy recipes, and reminders for her to take her iron supplement. Daniel no longer felt so lost, as he could refer his doubts to his friends who were already dads. "Feeling well supported during pregnancy can offer a sense of connection and belonging, as well as emotional comfort and reassurance, which can help you manage any worries or concerns that may arise," explains psychologist and pregnant health support Dr. Lauren Rockliffe (2023).

Social support networks are even more important for single moms. Without social connection, they risk feeling isolated, anxious, or depressed, and they find it harder to go through the prenatal visit schedule and adopt a healthy lifestyle. Although Juliet and Daniel had each other, they found their social support improved their pregnancy journey in every sense. "Having people around you who have been through the same experience can also be helpful when trying to adjust to your changing body, as they can offer advice on how to deal with the physical and emotional changes" (Rockliffe, 2023).

Sharing the joy of their pregnancy is one of the reasons why the second trimester is the best stage for many couples. The woman experiences relief from the first trimester's most annoying symptoms as her body adjusts to the pregnancy. She enjoys showing off her growing belly and becomes more confident in her capability of carrying a healthy baby as the chances of miscarriage significantly decrease. For many couples, the second trimester is also the time to know about the sex of the baby, which is exciting as you get to imagine this new person that will change your life forever, think of a name, and dream of the approaching day when you will hold him or her in your loving arms. We'll see all about this second stage in this chapter.

WHAT HAPPENS IN...

Your future baby, now officially a fetus, already has most of its organs and body parts but still needs to grow exponentially to be able to survive outside the uterus. Here are the major changes the baby and the mother experience during the second trimester:

Weeks 14 to 17

By the time the fourth month of the pregnancy begins, the baby is moving constantly inside the uterus, although it's still too early for the mother to feel these movements. Baby's body grows from the size of a small orange to the size of a big onion, and it starts to get covered in a soft layer of hair (called lanugo), which protects it and helps maintain the right temperature. Their facial features are slowly moving into place. By week 15, the ears are positioned by the sides of the head, and the eyes are also migrating to their final position. By week 16, they are already sensitive to light. Babies in week 17 are very active, practicing breathing movements, sucking, swallowing, and holding their neck straighter than before. Soon, your partner will be able to feel them as a tiny fish swimming inside her.

For many women, this is the time when fatigue, morning sickness, and other unpleasant first-trimester symptoms finally vanish. Your partner will feel more energetic and enjoy walks—for example, when shopping for maternity clothes! But if she still looks pretty slim, don't worry. Not every woman shows a fully popped pregnant belly yet. However, even if she's feeling great, she still needs to take good care of herself. Her immune system relaxes during pregnancy, and she's more prone to getting sick. Make sure your partner gets the flu shot, and if she gets a little under the weather, don't hesitate to call the doctor. She can take many medicines which are compatible with the pregnancy, but she should only take them when prescribed.

The second trimester is usually easier than the first and the last one. However, believe your partner if she says she isn't feeling like herself. Some second-trimester typical symptoms include back pain, round ligament pain, a stuffy nose, heartburn, and indigestion. Discuss these symptoms at your following prenatal appointment, as most can be relieved. You can also suggest your partner schedule a dentist appointment. "Hormones can affect the gums, ligaments, and bones in your mouth, which in turn can slightly loosen the teeth, especially if you have more serious untreated conditions like gingivitis or periodontitis" (Donaldson-Evans, 2023b).

Weeks 18 to 22

The fifth month of pregnancy is an exciting time for many parents-to-be because they finally get to find out whether they are having a boy or a girl! By week 18, genitals become visible so doctors can tell you the result on your next ultrasound... unless your little one decides to play a little hide-and-seek! Doctors will also tell whether all the organs are developing appropriately. On the screen, you could also catch your baby yawning or hiccupping!

Between 18 and 22 weeks, most women begin to feel the baby's movements. First, it may seem like a little rumble inside the belly that could be mistaken for gas. But as days go by, the little kicks become more noticeable. When your baby isn't sleeping, they practice grabbing, tasting what your partner feasts on, and listening to your voice with their developing sense of hearing. It's such an exciting time!

Around halfway through the pregnancy, your baby is still quite tiny. By week 20, they weigh just 10 ounces, but don't worry—they are growing fast! By week 22, most babies break the 1-pound mark. Their skin is covered in a cheesy varnish called vernix caseosa that protects it from the surrounding amniotic fluid. Some babies are born covered in that substance, which isn't appealing, but it's normal and healthy.

Your partner is probably showing a noticeable pregnant belly as her uterus grows. It has become so large that it's starting to shift the center of gravity, which may cause back pain as it pulls your partner's lower back forward. At the same time, the growing uterus pulls up the stomach, so heartburn and indigestion become more frequent. Remind your partner to eat her food slowly and sit down while you do the dishes. She should also increase her fiber intake to prevent constipation since digestion becomes slower. She should take things easy, as she's probably not sleeping peacefully every night. Leg cramps become annoying, and the pain from them can wake her up.

Her appetite is probably at its best. The doctor will control her weight gain to make sure it's within a normal range. Her stomach isn't the only growing body part; her feet sometimes expand into a new shoe size! She may like some changes better than others—but for the love of God, you always tell her she looks glowing and beautiful, no matter what the scale says. Between us dads, if you are caring and romantic, she'll show you her appreciation! This second trimester may be a honeymoon for you since many women recover their sex drive, and the baby belly still allows most of the sex positions. Enjoy being together! Once the baby is born, intimacy will have to wait.

Weeks 23 to 27

As the pregnancy approaches the end of the second trimester, your baby prepares for a significant growth spurt, in which they'll double their size in about a month. At the same time, your partner may experience considerable weight gain to support all this development. By week 23, your baby's skin is transparent and saggy, but soon, fat tissue will deposit inside their body to give them that lovely chubby newborn appearance they'll have three months later when they are finally born. By week 24, their facial features are already more defined—from this time onward, you could have a hint on who your baby resembles by having a 4D or 5D sonogram. By week 26, the baby opens their eyes. If you shine a flashlight in your partner's belly, you can sense some response from the inside!

During weeks 25 to 27, your baby's lungs quickly develop to allow them to breathe once they get outside the uterus. In fact, if, for some reason, a baby was born this early during pregnancy, they have a slight chance of surviving, although it would take a lot of time in the neonatal intensive care unit (NICU).

Just as your unborn baby experiences many changes this month so does your partner. She's probably gaining weight, which may cause her skin to stretch, creating itchiness and possibly some stretch marks. She can prevent some of them by applying moisturizer. And since we are talking about her skin, other changes due to pregnancy are the dark line that runs through her belly (from the belly button to the pubic area), known as the linea nigra. She should also protect herself from sunlight, as some women tend to get spots on their faces, and sunburn would make them permanent.

"Mommy brain" is a real thing! Not getting enough sleep, being anxious about the delivery date approaching, and physical changes can cause your partner to become more distracted and clumsy. Go easy on her! Other symptoms she can experience are red, itchy palms, swelling of her feet and legs (and other body parts as well! Some pregnant women deal with the discomfort of hemorrhoids), or changes in her vision. Although most of these symptoms are compatible with a healthy, normal pregnancy, make sure to discuss them with the health care provider during the prenatal appointments.

Mother's Physical and Emotional Changes

Most women describe the second trimester as the best part of their pregnancy. Their bodies are already adjusting to hormonal changes—though this doesn't mean they don't experience some uncomfortable symptoms—and since they share the news and begin to show, they usually receive sympathy and support from their friends, family, and coworkers.

As the pregnancy continues to develop, it gets easier to imagine the baby you will have in a few months (although, believe me, babies are never exactly as you imagined them; your child will always surprise you!). It's a great time to talk about baby names and to have long talks about parenting styles, education, and how the two of you will team up to give this child a great family environment.

While your partner is more energetic and in a better mood than the previous trimester, keep pampering her and make sure she doesn't take up additional efforts. If she's feeling fine, take advantage of these weeks and go out just the two of you! Go see a movie, eat at her favorite restaurant, or take a brief "babymoon" somewhere romantic. Pretty soon, date nights are going to become way more complicated!

WHAT YOU SHOULD KNOW...

During the second trimester, the doctor will continue to check your partner's health and perform a series of tests. These tests aren't just for confirming that all is well with your baby but also to detect and prevent possible health conditions that can happen in the second part of the pregnancy, such as gestational diabetes or high blood pressure. This is also the stage to start considering the birth plan. Let's have a closer look at what it means.

Birth Plan

Perhaps you're wondering what exactly a birth plan is. As the name indicates, it's a written outline where the pregnant woman (and her partner) list down her choices when it comes to labor day regarding the details of the type of birth she looks forward to, the procedures she would like to have done (if any), and overall her preferences for before, during, and after childbirth. Coming up with a birth plan is, for many couples, a way to empower themselves before the delivery day and to find out about the many choices available—as long as the pregnancy and delivery are without complications.

While it isn't mandatory to come up with a birth plan, it's always a good idea to discuss the details with your doctor, and it's advisable to have the plan written if several professionals are attending the birth. You could print copies of the birth plan to ensure they align with your partner's desires. She may leave some details blank if she's uncertain. For example, she may not be sure how she feels about being given an epidural. Maybe she can control the pain with relaxation and breathing techniques, but she wants to have the choice in case it becomes unbearable. That's also okay!

Just keep in mind that no birth plan is written in stone. Your partner may change her mind regarding specific preferences—and she should be listened to! Besides, doctors may indicate certain procedures if any complication arises during later pregnancy stages or labor. The birth plan displays the best-case scenario, but the hospital where you decide to give birth may allow or deny some of your preferences. Jennifer Geddes, from *What to Expect*, puts it this way: "The most important part of a good birth plan is flexibility. Childbirth is unpredictable. The best-laid plans don't always go, well, according to plan" (2021).

Tests and What They Do

If your partner stays healthy and no unexpected complications appear during the second trimester, her doctor will still want to check on her every month. Additionally, during this stage, the following tests will be suggested:

- **Routine tests:** The doctor will check your partner's weight and blood pressure and periodically test her urine, looking for protein, sugar, or any kind of infection. Plus, the height of the uterus (or fundal height) is measured to confirm the baby's growth, and the baby's heart can be heard with a hand-held ultrasound device.
- **Midtrimester ultrasound (the 18 to 20-week scan):** This is an exciting ultrasound because, for many couples, it's when they learn about the sex of the baby they're expecting. However, you should keep in mind it's a major medical study done for many reasons, so you shouldn't skip it even if you want to keep the sex a surprise until birth. Doctors perform the second-trimester sonogram to confirm the due date, examine the anatomy of the fetus and its blood flow patterns, check the amount of amniotic fluid, observe fetal activity and behavior, measure the length of your partner's cervix, monitor fetal growth, and see where the placenta is located.
- **Glucose screening:** Even healthy women have the chance of developing diabetes during their pregnancy; that's why doctors recommend this one-hour glucose tolerance exam. Your partner will drink a sugar solution and get her blood

tested an hour afterward. Further exams may be indicated if any abnormal blood sugar level appears. It's worth noticing that gestational diabetes can be treated with diet, exercise, and medication, and it usually goes away shortly after delivery.

- **Multiple marker tests/AFP4 screen/quad screen:** It's another blood test that tracks certain blood substances that indicate the risk—not the certainty—of chromosomic abnormalities. If the test comes out positive, doctors may suggest the following:
- **Amniocentesis:** It consists of the analysis of amniotic fluid the doctor extracts by inserting a needle through the abdomen into the amniotic sac. By studying the fetal cells contained in the fluid, doctors can tell almost for sure if the fetus has any genetic disorder or a neural tube defect. This test isn't performed in every pregnancy, only if some abnormalities were found on the NIPT in the first trimester, on the AFP in the second trimester, or if your partner has higher chances of carrying a baby with a congenital disability or a chromosomic disease. It's usually done between weeks 15 and 20, and while doctors may suggest it, it's up to you as a couple to discuss its pros and cons because it's invasive and carries a small risk of losing the pregnancy. For example, if you decide you'll still carry on with the pregnancy if the fetus is at risk of having Down Syndrome, you may decide against amniocentesis.

WHAT YOU CAN DO...

As the pregnancy develops, your role continues to be important! Besides discussing with your partner the pros and cons of medical tests and coming up with a birth plan, there are many ways you can support her during this stage.

Support Your Partner

Here's what your partner would love you to do:

- **Give her a massage:** The ligaments in her body naturally become softer. If your partner complains about lower back pain, a gentle massage could help her feel better. Remind her to put her feet up to relieve swollen ankles. "A massage can melt away pregnancy aches and pains. It may also help you relax and sleep better" (Pathak, 2021).
- **Relieve her headaches:** Many women experience migraine or headaches during pregnancy. Give her paracetamol, which is perfectly safe, and try to relieve any stress in her daily routine.
- **Tell her she looks amazing:** Your partner may be concerned about all her physical changes during this stage. Be reassuring and supportive about her appearance.
- **Have sex with her:** Many women feel friskier during the second trimester! Don't be afraid to hurt your partner or the baby. Unless your doctor advises against it, sex during pregnancy is safe and pleasurable for both of you. As the belly grows, make sure your partner is comfortable. "If sex is uncomfortable right now, try new positions. Lie on your side or try getting on your hands and knees to accommodate your growing belly" (Pathak, 2021).
- **Research childbirth classes:** Soon, you two will attend preparation for labor. Find out what your health provider offers and sign up. You can also take parenting or first-aid classes to feel better prepared for the baby's arrival.
- **Connect with your baby:** You can achieve this by talking or singing to them. By this stage, their hearing is already developing, which can help your baby get used to your

voice. Soon, you'll be able to feel their movements when placing a hand on the bump.

- **Paint the nursery:** Besides doing any heavy lifting, a chore you should definitely take on is decorating your baby's future room. Your partner shouldn't inhale any paint fumes or wallpaper glue.
- **Visit the hospital:** This is already a good time to explore the facilities of the place where you plan to have the baby. In some hospitals, you can already pre-register.

Baby's Sex and Names

When it comes to the baby's sex, which one is better? To find out or to wait? Some couples can't wait for the doctor to tell them whether the baby is a boy or a girl, while others decide to keep the secret until delivery. There's no right answer, and you and your partner must decide for yourselves. Keep in mind the following:

If You Decide to Know

Finding out alleviates some of the pregnant couple's anxiety. Many find they can better relate to the baby once they start picturing him or her according to the sex and giving the baby a name. Even if they expected the opposite, they still have many months to adjust their expectations. Plus, they get to decorate the nursery and get baby's clothing according to traditional styles for boys or girls. Finally, the fun of throwing a gender-reveal party with all blue or pink is yet another advantage.

It's not all pros, though. For a start, tests could be wrong, and you'll end up dressing a boy all in pink or a girl all in blue if they made a mistake, especially when friends and family usually put a lot of emphasis on traditional gender colors when buying gifts for the baby. Some couples believe it's better not to put so much emphasis on a child's sex, especially since gender roles depend on many other factors rather than biology. "While sex can be determined before birth, a person's gender is not typically chosen until childhood, adolescence, or beyond" (Terreri, 2017).

If You Keep Baby's Sex a Secret

Some couples love the element of surprise! They choose two or more names for the baby and decorate the nursery in neutral tones such as green or yellow. They refrain from assigning their unborn baby stereotypical traits regarding their sex and ask their friends and family for gender-neutral clothes. There's no chance of disappointment when you find out if you are already holding a newborn.

The cons of not knowing are mainly dealing with societal pressures. Your friends and family may drive you crazy, and their disappointment of not knowing may be hard to deal with.

What if your partner wants to keep the secret, but you desperately need to know, or the other way around? While some people may be okay with one of them talking to the doctor in private and keeping the news for themselves, it's probably better to communicate honestly and reach for a joint decision. Accidentally spilling the beans may be a source of conflict within the couple.

Tips for Choosing Names

Maybe you've decided on your baby's name way before trying to get pregnant. Or perhaps now your baby is on the way, you feel overwhelmed with name suggestions from everyone around you! How can you pick the perfect name for your baby? Here are some suggestions:

- **Sources of inspiration:** You may find a great name inspired by a location, someone from pop culture, or your cultural inheritance. Of course, if you are more comfortable sticking to a religious name or carrying on a family tradition, that's great, too!
- **Alphabetical lists:** How about choosing the initials before the name? From there, you can check out alphabetical lists online and find the best name for a boy or a girl that better goes with the last name(s) the baby will carry.
- **Reasons for having a middle name:** While many people don't find any practical use in having a middle name, it can come in handy for "hiding" that traditional family name you don't adore, for allowing yourselves to be playful— John Legolas Smith? Why not? Or for giving your child a chance in the future in case they don't share your preference for their first name.
- **Can you choose a last name?** Depending on where your baby is born, you may or may not choose the baby's last name. In some states or countries, giving the child their father's last name is mandatory if it's known. Other people choose to use both the dad's and the mom's last names, whether hyphenating them or combining them into a new last name (Murray, 2023).
- **Watch out for nicknames and difficult spellings:** When considering names, check out potential nicknames and see if they match both the middle and the last names and don't sound funny. Regarding spelling, you need to find a balance between giving your child a unique name and creating a future nightmare at school when their teachers get it wrong every single time.

INTERACTIVE ELEMENT: COME UP WITH THE RIGHT BIRTH PLAN

If you and your partner haven't created a birth plan yet, here are some questions you should ask yourselves to include in the outline. Afterward, you can either have it written or simply discuss the details with your health provider. Remember, any birth plan is only a guideline based on your partner's preferences, but the ultimate goal is to deliver the baby in the safest way possible for both mother and child.

- If given the choice, which type of childbirth would you prefer?
- Where do you want to give birth? At home or in a hospital facility?
- Would you like to be able to move around, drink fluids, and play music during labor?
- How would you like to control the pain? Would you like to be given anesthesia?
- Who should be allowed to be in your room during labor?
- Which elements would you like to try during labor? (a birthing ball, birthing chair, bathtub, etc.)
- Do you have a birthing position of preference?
- Do you agree with using a catheter or an enema?
- Are you okay with having permanent fetal monitoring/rupture of the membranes/an episiotomy?
- Do you plan to store/donate umbilical cord blood?
- Do you allow pictures/videos during delivery? Who should take them?
- Who is going to hold the baby/cut the umbilical cord/go with the baby when they have the medical procedures done?
- If your baby is a boy, will you have him circumcised?

- Do you plan to breastfeed or bottle-feed?
- Would you rather have the baby stay in your room or a nursery if available?

KEY TAKEAWAYS

We've learned about what to expect during the second trimester. In addition to following up on prenatal visits, remember the importance of building a support group with your friends and family, coming up with baby names, and coming up with a birth plan. In the following chapter, we'll discuss the third trimester.

HELP FUTURE DADS NAVIGATE THE JOURNEY

Embrace the Gift of Guidance

"The best way to find yourself is to lose yourself in the service of others."

— *MAHATMA GANDHI*

Those who share wisdom with no expectation of reward often find greater fulfillment and joy in life. So, why not give it a shot?

To kickstart that journey, let me pose a question...

Would you lend a hand to someone you've never met, even if you never received recognition for it?

Who might this person be, you wonder? They're akin to you. Or, at least, to the version of you from yesteryears. Eager but uncertain, craving to make a difference, yet unsure where to turn.

My aim? To simplify the journey of impending fatherhood for dads everywhere. Every effort I exert stems from this purpose. And, the only way for me to achieve it is by reaching... well... everyone.

This is where you can play a pivotal role. As it turns out, many individuals do judge a book by its cover (and its reviews). So, here's my humble request on behalf of a struggling new dad you've yet to meet:

Would you kindly lend your voice by leaving a review for this book?

Simply scan the QR code below to leave your review:

Your contribution demands no monetary investment and merely a fraction of your time, yet it holds the potential to forever alter the trajectory of a fellow father's life. Your review might just...

Provide invaluable guidance during pregnancy, foster confidence, and strengthen familial bonds to positively impact a new dad's life.

To Leave A Review Go To:
https://bit.ly/123dad

- Or Scan Below -

THE THIRD TRIMESTER

As months went by and delivery day was approaching, Juliet and Daniel were very active decorating the nursery in shades of green—they chose not to find out about the baby's sex—purchasing baby gear (a stroller, crib, car seat, and other stuff they couldn't borrow), and following up with prenatal appointments and tests. It wasn't until week 34 that they started their childbirth classes, and that's because Juliet's ob-gyn told them to.

Daniel told me later that he felt a bit useless at first, realizing that everything about the birthing process was up to Juliet and Juliet alone. However, one good thing about attending the course was that he learned all about warning signs and how to tell if the baby was about to arrive. This came in handy when, one morning during breakfast, early in week 38, Juliet experienced a sudden back pain. Despite her complaints, Daniel rushed to get her to the hospital. Fortunately, they had packed the hospital bag a few nights before!

As the due date approaches, it's more important than ever to be prepared for the symptoms and be able to tell what's normal and what isn't. Your partner is likely to be uncomfortable in this last stage, and it's part of your duty to help her feel empowered and reassured about what's going to happen. Women are prepared to carry and deliver babies. She's got this, and you've got this, too! Let's find out what happens during the third trimester, the last stage of pregnancy.

WHAT HAPPENS IN...

By the time the pregnancy enters the third trimester, if you could peek at the fetus, you'd discover it already resembles a tiny baby with all its body parts and features. However, it's not yet time to be born; it still needs to grow and gain strength.

Weeks 28 to 32

During the seventh month of pregnancy, your baby spends a lot of time sleeping and dreaming—something specialists know because fetuses this age experience rapid eye movement (or REM), the stage of sleep when dreams happen. Their eyes remain closed most of the time, but they can blink them, and they already have eyelashes. Although your partner should feel them move several times a day, the baby isn't doing those spectacular acrobatics as before since the uterus is more cramped—and it's about to get even more so! By week 29, the baby's length is close to its birth size, but it still needs to double its weight. By the time the pregnancy reaches week 32, the baby will likely settle in the head-down position.

Your baby's brain, in particular, experiences huge changes during these weeks. Not only does it get bigger, but it also gets more wrinkled as it allows more room for brain tissue. The connections between brain cells are fundamental for supporting your baby once they are born, but even now, they allow your child to process information from their developing five senses.

Your partner is becoming a bit more uncomfortable as her belly grows, and she may experience annoying symptoms such as sciatica (tingling leg pain) and swollen blood vessels. She might not be able to sleep comfortably anymore as the baby is probably more active at nighttime, and the skin over her belly feels tight and itchy. Some of the symptoms of early pregnancy come back, such as frequent urination and heartburn, although now it's not because of the hormones but due to the pressure of the uterus on the other organs. This can also cause her to become short of breath, something that will improve once the baby's head drops down into her pelvis as they prepare for birth.

Weeks 33 to 37

As the middle of the trimester approaches, your baby has reached the length they'll measure once they are born, but by week 33, they are still putting on half a pound weekly. Although premature babies born during the eighth month of pregnancy have good chances of developing properly without any consequences, they should stay inside as long as possible, at least until week 37, when they are considered full-term babies.

During these weeks, besides gaining weight, your baby is developing their immune system, shedding the waxy coat that kept them protected the past months, growing their fingernails, and accumulating body fat and gray matter. All they have to do now is to practice for their life outside the uterus. They inhale and exhale amniotic fluid, swallow it, and suck their thumb.

Your partner is likely experiencing periodical Braxton-Hicks contractions, which are "practice" contractions. Unlike the real ones, they aren't painful and usually disappear when she changes her position. During birth classes, you will learn how to tell if it's time to go to the hospital or if you can still wait at home. By the time the baby drops, she'll start waddling and possibly experiencing some pelvic discomfort because of the pressure of the baby's head.

Weeks 38 to 42

It's the final countdown! By week 39, your baby is fully developed and could be born any time now. During the following days, they are shedding the lanugo, their skin has gained a pinkish to white appearance (the pigmentation occurs shortly after birth), and their eyes have turned the color they'll have at birth—although this may not be the permanent shade, as they may keep changing until baby's first birthday. By week 40, the ninth month of pregnancy is complete, although the two of you may feel it has lasted several years.

Besides anxiety, fear of labor, insomnia, and a strong nesting instinct, your partner may experience leaky breasts. They produce colostrum, which will be your baby's first food. She may also lose her mucus plug, a yellow or brownish discharge of a substance that has been keeping her cervix close but not anymore for obvious reasons. And no, it's not a sign that delivery is immediate, as it can be lost weeks prior!

What happens if the due date passes? Well, nothing! About 1 in 3 pregnancies hit the 41-week mark (Donaldson-Evans, 2023c). Babies aren't considered overdue until week 42 because their late check-up is probably a miscalculation of the original due date. However, if you reach this point, after careful monitoring, the baby's doctor will induce labor.

Mother's Physical and Emotional Changes

The last trimester of pregnancy is challenging for your partner. As the baby gains weight, so does she, and carrying such a big belly makes it hard for her to engage in simple daily tasks, such as riding public transportation, doing groceries, or even tying her shoelaces! She's not getting a good night's sleep (and she's not likely to get one any time soon!), and labor approaching can make her anxious.

With all these changes, she may not recognize herself in the mirror. Remind her that the transformation she's going through is part of the miracle of carrying a new life inside her, and tell her she glows. If she gives you a look of disbelief, praise her hair. Hormones are responsible for it growing longer, stronger, and falling much less, so it's a positive side effect of pregnancy!

You will insist on lifting heavy stuff and telling her to get some rest, but if she's often seen around the house emptying cupboards or vacuuming the floors, that's not because she lost it. It's a natural consequence of pregnancy called the nesting instinct. While it can be useful to finish setting up the nursery or pre-washing all those lovely baby clothes she got at her baby shower, remind her not to overdo it. She needs to save some energy for the big day!

WHAT YOU SHOULD KNOW...

With the delivery day approaching, you and your partner are up to more frequent checkups and medical tests. Besides, this is an excellent time to interview pediatricians for your baby.

Your Baby's Doctor

Three months before the due date is a great time to start searching for a pediatrician for your child. This isn't a matter to be taken lightly, as their doctor will be the most important person to look after your child's health for their entire childhood and adolescence. Not only do they see children when they are sick, but they also monitor their growth and development, offer answers regarding sleep and feeding, and perform immunizations.

You should fully trust your baby's doctor and feel secure with their advice and guidance. Alanna Nuñez, from *What to Expect*, believes a pediatrician is more than your baby's doctor because even when they are there to prescribe cough medicine or flu shots, they "will also be there to answer your questions about postpartum depression or anxiety and assure you on the bad days that you're actually doing a good job at this whole parenting-a-new-human-being-thing" (Nuñez, 2022). Therefore, you need to find someone who aligns with your family's values. If you haven't met them yet, you are likely to have more than one interview until you find the right health professional for your family.

To start your search, you can ask for recommendations from your friends and family and then check with your insurance to see if any of those doctors are in your plan. Additionally, you can read online reviews of professionals in your area. You can opt for a pediatrician or a family physician, who treats patients of all ages. Of course, whoever you choose, you need to make sure they are board-certified, meaning they are fully qualified to treat your baby.

How can you decide between a couple (or several) of highly qualified doctors? How can you tell who the right professional is for you and your baby? Here are some tips:

- **Proximity:** You'll need to check up on your baby several times, especially during the first year, as doctors monitor their growth. If you have to drive an hour to the doctor's office, it will become an inconvenience, even if you have an emergency room nearby.

- **Availability:** When is the doctor available? Are they part of a team, and could other doctors or nurses check on your baby if they were temporarily unavailable? Do they accept video calls? Do they offer schedules on the weekends and evenings? Who should you call when the doctor is on vacation? How should you handle emergencies?
- **Costs:** How much will you pay after each visit? Does your insurance cover at least part of it? Must you pay in full each time, or can you pay over time if necessary?
- **Values:** Make sure your doctor's views align with yours regarding breastfeeding or bottle-feeding, co-sleeping, vaccines, antibiotics, potty training, circumcision, and any other aspect you and your partner find important.
- **Environment:** During your interview, check the waiting room. Is it child-friendly? How long do the other families have to wait? Is the office clean and tidy?
- **Treatment:** How do you feel during the interview? Does the doctor take the time to answer all of your questions, or do they seem in a rush? Are they clear and respectful, or do they use a condescending tone? The right professional will feel right. More than their credentials, you need to listen to your gut!

Prenatal Appointments, Tests, and What They Do

Before taking your baby to the pediatrician, your partner must bring them into the world! During this last stage of pregnancy, she's expected to attend more frequent prenatal appointments. By the time she gets to week 28, the doctor will ask her to come every two weeks, and as the due date approaches, from week 36 onwards, every week. While it may sound like you'll spend a lot of time around the doctor's office, these close checkups usually reassure many expecting couples.

During the appointments, the now usual controls take place. The doctor will measure your partner's weight and blood pressure, as well as the size of her belly, and listen to the baby's heartbeat. Sometimes, they request a urine sample or indicate further studies, especially if yours is a high-risk pregnancy. For example, if your partner develops common pregnancy-related diseases such as preeclampsia or gestational diabetes, a third-trimester sonogram will be necessary to make sure the baby's growth and development are adequate. Additionally, if a previous ultrasound showed placenta previa (when the placenta partially or totally covers the cervix), doctors need to check whether the problem has been resolved or if it's necessary to program a C-section.

If your partner tests Rh-negative, she will receive an injection of Rh immune globulin that prevents her body from producing antibodies, something that could be bad news if your baby is Rh-positive.

Between 35 and 37 weeks, there's a painless yet uncomfortable test of group B strep. Your partner needs to have her anus and vagina swabbed to check for a common infection. If the results are positive, she is treated with antibiotics to prevent the baby being infected during labor.

Once your partner is past her due date, doctors may suggest a cervical check to see if it's softening, which could indicate labor is approaching. The baby's heartbeat and fetal activity are also monitored closely to ensure the pregnancy can continue until labor begins naturally. This can be done through a nonstress test (NST) or—less likely—a contraction stress test (CST) to see if the baby responds accordingly to stimulation.

Of course, prenatal appointments are the best place to talk about your partner's symptoms and ask any necessary questions you may have now that the final day is approaching. However, certain symptoms require you to call the doctor right away. These include:

- bleeding
- increased vaginal discharge that smells
- fever
- pain when she pees
- intense headache or blind spots in her eyesight
- sudden swelling or weight gain
- trouble breathing
- regular, painful contractions
- the baby isn't moving as often
- her water breaks

Antenatal Classes

Although you'll only learn to be a father by experience, it's a good idea to take some classes to feel empowered and help you get ready for what's ahead: mostly labor, birth, feeding a baby, and taking care of them during the first few months. These classes are known as antenatal classes, labor classes, or birthing classes, and both pregnant women and their partners may find it helpful to take them.

Antenatal classes usually take about eight hours to cover all the important topics. Since they revolve around the busy schedule of expecting couples, you take the course over several weeks. Therefore, it's a good idea to sign up for it when you enter the third trimester, around week 28 (or even earlier if you're expecting twins!). You can ask your partner's doctor or health provider for recommendations. You should also check with your health insurance company to see if they cover the cost of the class. Sometimes, you can find these classes in hospitals, charities, or private practices. However, the person who imparts them doesn't need to be a doctor. Doulas can teach private antenatal classes as well.

Which topics are covered in these classes? Here are some for you to get an idea:

- how to follow a healthy diet and lifestyle during pregnancy
- exercises for your partner on the last stage of the trimester
- what to expect during labor and birth
- relaxation techniques for natural birthing and pain relief
- information about the different possible interventions in childbirth, including what happens during a C-section
- when to go to the hospital
- how to take care of a newborn
- tips for breastfeeding
- what to expect for postpartum, including warning signs
- feelings and emotions before, during, and after childbirth

There's not a single type of antenatal class. You may find the traditional course available together with other options, such as Lamaze, hypnobirthing, antenatal yoga or Pilates, or active birth, so make sure you explore different choices with your partner and find the one that better suits you. Some of them provide a general overview of all the aforementioned topics, while others are centered on something more specific, such as active movement during labor or breathing techniques to control pain without drugs.

Other than finding answers to your most common questions, these classes provide an opportunity to meet other expecting couples, which can be great for expanding your support group. "Friends made at antenatal classes often meet with each other through the first few months with their new baby and can be a great source of support for each other" (*Antenatal Classes*, n.d.).

Hospital Bag

As your due date approaches, you need to make sure your partner has everything she needs for when the time comes to go to the hospital. Some women prepare the bag as early as week 33, while others decide to wait, but it's always better not to wait until the last minute. Remind your partner to have the hospital bag all packed by week 38 since the baby could be born any day then, and you don't want to rush things.

The length of the hospital stay depends on whether your partner has a vaginal delivery or a C-section. In the first case, she'll usually get admitted for two days, and in the second, maybe three or four.

What should you pack? While it's always a good idea to check with her doctor or the facility where she's going to have the baby which items she's requested to bring along, here is a checklist of the essentials:

For the Mom-To-Be

- **Documents:** Bring a photo ID or driver's license, insurance info, hospital paperwork, and one or more copies of the birth plan you created.
- **Clothes:** Pack pajamas, warm socks, a comfy robe or a sweater, maternity bras, underwear that can fit big pads, and loose clothes for going back home.
- **Toiletries:** While the hospital will probably provide essential items such as maxi pads, soap, and shampoo, she may want to pack her own. Include a hairbrush or a comb, deodorant, toothbrush and toothpaste, lotion, lip balm,

and nursing pads. If she's receiving visits, she may want to have some makeup.

- **Personal items:** Bring her cell phone and charger, glasses or contact lenses, headbands, clips, or scrunchy, music and headphones, snacks for eating after labor, and some diversions for long labor, such as magazines, video games, or a fun book.

For the Baby

While the hospital usually provides everything the baby needs during their stay (including clothes, diapers, and wipes), you must remember the following essentials:

- **Infant car seat:** Have this device properly installed.
- **Clothes for coming back home:** Bring a onesie, socks, a hat, and extra layers of clothing depending on the weather —but don't overdress the baby! If they are born in the summer and it's 87 °F out there, they don't need a tiny jacket!
- **Pediatrician information:** It's a good idea to include their contact numbers and information for the hospital nurses.
- **Bottles:** If you plan to bottle-feed, make sure you include them in the hospital bag as well.

For You

- **Clothes:** Think as if you were taking a short trip! Take your pajamas, a T-shirt, extra socks, and underwear.
- **Toiletries:** Bring your shampoo, deodorant, toothbrush, toothpaste, contact lenses and solution, etc.
- **Snacks:** Bring a selection of snacks, reusable bottles, and lots of change for the hospital vending machines.

- **Entertainment:** Plan music, light reading material, your laptop, a deck of cards, and whatever items help you make the waiting hours shorter.
- **Camera and an extra battery:** Be ready to capture the first memories together.
- **Cell phone and charger:** Make sure you have the contact information for everyone you want to share the news with, too!
- **A lightweight pillow:** This will come in handy if you are planning to stay overnight.

WHAT YOU CAN DO...

By this time, your partner is feeling exhausted, heavy, and uncomfortable, and she probably can't wait for the pregnancy to finally be over—and to welcome the baby, of course! Here's how you can help her thrive:

Support Your Partner

- **Let her rest:** She's getting up several times a night to pee and can't find a comfortable position. Let her sleep as much as possible and do the household chores yourself.
- **Be her driver:** Even if she insists she can walk somewhere, offer to drive her around so she doesn't need to waddle.
- **Connect with your baby:** Talk to them, sing to them, and touch the belly.
- **Understand her moods:** Your partner's sex drive is usually lower now since she's experiencing discomfort and can't recognize her body. Be sympathetic, and replace love-making with cuddles and massages.

- **Install the car seat:** You must have the device properly installed and checked to ensure that you can drive the baby home safely. Do it ahead of time!
- **Help her pack:** Use the hospital bag list provided earlier in this chapter.
- **Stock up the freezer:** Cook ahead for the first days at home with the newborn. Things are going to be crazy!
- **Learn the fastest route:** Study your map for when the time comes to take her to the hospital.
- **Do fun stuff together:** The time being just the two of you is almost over as you're about to become a family. Make the best of your last weeks as a single couple with no kids!
- **Pre-register at the hospital:** Help your partner with all the necessary paperwork in advance so that when the day comes, you won't have to increase your anxiety by filling out any forms.

Nursery Room and Essentials

The first time you have a baby, you may feel overwhelmed when you learn about the huge stock of baby gear you'll need to buy. Take a deep breath, call your friends and family to let them know you've registered, and get some second-hand or borrowed items if you are on a tight budget.

Some couples decide to start decorating the baby's nursery during their pregnancy, while others wait until after the baby is born, either because they are still to find out about the baby's sex or because they are planning to share their room with the baby for the first months. Remember that if you are planning on painting and setting up a room, that's a whole lot of work and you'll hardly have the time to do it while taking care of a newborn, so my suggestion is to at least start ahead!

If possible, choose a calm, quiet space with natural light for your baby. Keep the baby close to your bedroom so you don't have to walk around the house when they get you up at night. Choose light colors for the walls, curtains, and ceiling, and avoid carpets, which can cause allergies. Most importantly: Make sure the nursery is completely safe for the baby! Have an electrician check sockets and wiring, attach furniture to the wall to prevent the baby from accidentally knocking anything down, and baby-proof the space.

INTERACTIVE ELEMENT: BABY CHECKLIST

What do you need to buy for your baby? Some items are truly basic, while others can be included on your wish list, but you can do without them. Some are for right away (like the mandatory car seat) and others can wait (your baby won't need a chair until they are 4 or 5 months old). Here's a checklist for you to decide which items to buy, borrow, or ask for a present:

- crib or cradle
- firm, flat mattress
- 3–4 sets of fitted crib sheets
- chest of drawers or a baby wardrobe
- changing table and cleaning supplies (diapers, wipes, diaper cream, cotton, etc.)
- comfortable chair for your partner to sit and feed the baby
- baby monitor
- play mat
- toy chest or basket
- baby bathtub plus shampoo, body wash, and soft towels

KEY TAKEAWAYS

We've seen how the third trimester can be uncomfortable for your partner and a source of anxiety for both as you prepare to welcome your baby. Taking antenatal classes, packing the hospital bag, and enjoying the time spent together are great ways to make these weeks go faster. Before you know it, the big day has arrived! Let's read about delivery in the next chapter.

IT'S THE DAY

That morning, while she was having breakfast, Juliet experienced a sudden pain in the back. Daniel remembered something the doula had told them during antenatal classes. "What if it's a contraction?" he said. Although Juliet felt it was still early for delivery since her due date was two weeks later, they both agreed to get a check-up at the hospital just in case. Daniel put the hospital bag in the trunk of the car and breathed in relief as he noticed the baby car seat he had already installed. While he drove her through one of the three routes he had practiced, Juliet took advantage of those minutes to go through her birth plan once more.

I wish I had known as much as him when I became a dad for the first time! My wife's water broke in the middle of the night. Back then, cell phones weren't as common, and we didn't have the doctor's number, so we had to call him home and wake him up. He told us she shouldn't wait and he'd meet us at the hospital. That's when I remembered I'd never driven there before! And there wasn't a GPS to guide me! To make things worse, we hadn't made arrangements for the neighbor to feed our dog, so that's another person we had to get out of bed before sunrise.

As you can see, when delivery day comes, you can't have everything under control, but the more you can plan, the fewer reasons you'll have to stress about so you can focus on what's really important: taking care of your partner and get ready to meet your baby. Let's go through the basics of what you'll get through that day!

WHAT HAPPENS WHEN...

By the time the big day arrives, you'll feel more confident knowing you are prepared. This doesn't mean everything will go exactly as you plan! For example, your partner may decide she does want an epidural in the end because the pain is too much to handle. Doctors could decide it's better to opt for a C-section because the baby moved, and it's not in the best position for a vaginal delivery. Or, labor could last for hours and hours! That's why flexibility is the key to success. It will help you stay calm and strong to better support your partner when she needs you the most.

It's Time

With the impressive list of symptoms women have during each stage of pregnancy, you may wonder whether you or your partner will be able to recognize if labor has finally started. How can you tell some other random pregnancy discomfort from the real thing? Some specific signals indicate the due date is approaching, but there's no rush to get to the hospital yet. These include:

- **Dilation and cervix change:** During the cervical exam, doctors will check on your partner to notice any early signs of labor. Near the delivery date, the cervix becomes softer and thinner. During delivery, it will dilate up to 10 centimeters to allow the baby to go out.

- **Braxton Hicks:** Your partner may have been feeling them all the second half of the pregnancy, but they become more often and more intense in the end. The main difference with real contractions is their frequency, intensity, and location. Unlike real contractions, Braxton Hicks ones are irregular and decrease when your partner changes her position. When in doubt, ask her to sit or lie down for a while.
- **Stomach issues:** Although indigestion and heartburn are common pregnancy symptoms, pay attention if your partner has a sudden bout of diarrhea or nausea, as some women experience them 48 to 24 hours before labor begins (Health Partners, 2021). According to certified midwife Rachel Lieberman, "That's the body's way of emptying the bowels so the uterus will contract well" (Stein et al., 2022).
- **Losing the mucus plug:** Your partner may notice a single mucus-like discharge coming from her vagina or an increment in her usual discharge. However, some women lose the plug days or even weeks before giving birth, and some others don't notice it at all.
- **Loose-feeling joints:** This is due to the increment of the hormone relaxin, which is good news for the pelvis as it will stay flexible and stretch, but bad news for your partner as she feels uncomfortable, clumsy, and wobbly.
- **Baby drops:** The baby starts descending the birth canal, which creates pelvic pressure, but a positive side effect is a relief in the diaphragm and easier breathing for your partner.
- **No more weight gain:** The baby has reached their birth size, and there's less amniotic fluid than a few weeks ago.

In her next weekly check-up, your partner may be
surprised that she weighs the same as the previous week.

As the due date arrives, here are the signs and symptoms to watch
for. If any of these happen, then yes, by all means, take your
partner to the hospital and carry the bag with you because it's baby
time:

- **Real contractions:** Early labor contractions are mild and
  irregular, similar to Braxton-Hicks, but they become more
  intense and frequent as your partner advances towards
  active labor. That's why it's a good idea to time
  contractions and the intervals between them. You can use
  an app or the stopwatch from your phone. How do they
  feel? Tell her they'll remind her of intense menstrual
  cramps.
- **Consistent pain in the lower back or belly:** Although
  backache is normal to some degree during the late stages
  of pregnancy, some women experience pain or cramping
  in their lower backs that move in waves toward the front.
  They are most likely labor contractions. Additionally, the
  way the baby is placed can influence where your partner
  feels more pain. There's something called "back labor" pain
  that happens when the baby's head puts pressure on the
  mother's tailbone and spine (Health Partners, 2021).
- **Bloody show:** If her increment in vaginal discharge comes
  in pinkish or brownish tones, it's a good indicator of the
  cervix changes and labor imminently approaching.
- **The water breaks:** It's the typical scenario you picture,
  and I blame romantic comedies! You and your partner are
  enjoying a candlelight dinner when suddenly... splash! She
  spills water like a balloon. In real life, your partner is more
  likely to experience this in the final moments of labor,

already in the hospital. "For most women, membranes rupture, and amniotic fluid leaks after other labor symptoms have already begun. And you won't necessarily lose it all in one big gush, either—for some women, water breaking feels more like a trickle" (Donaldson-Evans, 2021). Water breaking is, nonetheless, an irreversible sign of labor, so you should head to the hospital anyway.

Additionally, always call the doctor (no matter how far your partner is into the pregnancy) if she experiences:

- **Bleeding or a bright red discharge:** Unlike the pink or brownish bloody show, this is a sign of a problem, and your partner should get immediate medical treatment.
- **Water comes out green or brown**: These colors indicate the presence of meconium, your baby's first stool, which can be dangerous if they ingest it. Labor must happen, and it must happen fast.
- **Blurred or double vision:** It's a common sign of preeclampsia, pregnancy-induced high blood pressure, which has to be treated right away. If the pregnancy is full-term, doctors may opt for inducing labor.
- **Severe headache:** A mild headache that goes away with Tylenol (acetaminophen) can be due to her anxiety and lack of a proper night's sleep. But a sudden, intense headache can also be a symptom of high blood pressure.
- **Sudden swelling:** Another common sign of preeclampsia to watch out for.

It's normal for couples to rush to the hospital when there's still plenty of time, especially if this is their first baby. Sometimes, they are told to go home after checking everything is okay, and it can be disappointing to come back with still no baby. But don't let this fear keep you from having your partner checked if you have any doubts! It's better to be safe than sorry.

You Arrive in the Hospital

Before going to the hospital, check with your partner's ob-gyn or midwife. They'll be able to tell if you need to rush or if there's still time. Finally, they tell you to take her there. You were able to spot the signals and remember the fastest route to the hospital or birthing center of choice. Luckily, you made it on time! No baby has come out of your partner's body yet, right? So far, so good. What should you do now?

In your hospital bag, you've packed insurance information, and you've probably filled in lots of paperwork the days before when you pre-registered, providing them with all the necessary information in advance about your partner, her medical history, her doctor, and your baby's doctor. But if your partner begins labor unexpectedly—in the case of premature birth—you'll have to fill in a lot of forms. In some cases, no matter how much you plan, the hospital staff may still ask you to do some paperwork or to fill out some more forms again. Take a deep breath and do it; don't overload your partner with your frustration!

Once you arrive at the hospital, it's a good idea to be familiarized with the different entrances. Instead of going to the emergency room (ER), you will take your partner to labor and delivery, provided that she's not experiencing some of the symptoms considered risky (such as strong bleeding or high blood pressure).

There, a nurse will take her to a triage room to evaluate how far she's into labor. Unless, of course, she comes in screaming, and she's obviously about to give birth! Additionally, if your partner is having a scheduled induction or C-section, the doctor will tell you when to arrive, and your partner will be admitted without triage.

Then, she'll have a fetal monitor hooked into her belly, a device that checks both the baby's heart rate and her contractions. Her cervix will also be checked to see if she has dilated. If her water hasn't broken yet and there are still no signs of progress, this is the point when you could be sent back home (Donovan Mauer, 2017). Never mind! You'll be back pretty soon. If there are labor contractions and some dilation, your partner will be admitted.

Once given a room, she'll have to change her clothes and wear a hospital gown. Take it easy; things could move slowly from here as contractions become more frequent and her cervix fully dilates! This is the moment when you take out your music and video games, the birth ball, the scented candles, or anything that can help her spend the hours as comfortably as possible. A nurse will periodically check on her to see how she and the baby are doing.

What happens afterward depends on whether she asked for an epidural, opioid IV medication, or no medication at all. With an epidural, she may need to wait for the anesthesiologist to arrive. After being administered, she won't be able to stand, so she will spend the rest of the waiting in bed, constantly monitored and being given fluids through an IV. If she waits before receiving it or straight skips medication, she can deal with the pain in natural ways, such as walking around, changing positions, taking a shower, and so on.

How long will you have to wait before the baby is born? Well, it's a long, long wait! Typically, labor takes about 12 to 18 hours if this is your first baby (*What to Expect in the Delivery Room*, n.d.). Don't expect the nurse to spend all her shift in the room with you and your partner. For most of the labor, the two of you will be on your own, with another person you decided to bring along, or with the doula if you hired one. Your partner's doctor isn't likely to check on her until it's almost showtime!

Delivery Room

As hours go by, contractions will become more intense and frequent. Don't be surprised if your partner decides she wants some pain relief after all! Soon, the cervix will be fully dilated (10 centimeters), and she will feel the urge to push. At this stage of active labor, she will receive the assistance of a nurse and either her doctor or midwife, who will tell her exactly when to push. This may take either a couple of attempts or a couple of hours—in any case, in the final push, they will guide the baby out of the birth canal and—there! You are finally a dad!

This is what happens if your partner has a vaginal birth and every-thing goes fine. However, if after long, painful contractions, your partner's cervix isn't dilating or if, when monitoring the baby, they notice any signs of fetal distress, doctors may indicate an emer-gency C-section. Reassure your partner that it is for the best! It doesn't matter if labor doesn't go according to plan as long as she and the baby are okay. Although a C-section is a surgery, it can still be a family-friendly experience and a celebration of bringing your child into the world.

C-Section

What happens during a C-section? The nurse will prepare your partner by removing any jewelry, shaving or clipping her pubic hair, and cleaning her skin with anti-bacterial wipes. She'll receive anesthesia—if she already had an epidural, she might be given an extra dose. General anesthesia, in which your partner is asleep, is only used in emergencies (1% of births), so most times, women are awake and fully conscious to receive their babies (*Unplanned*

Cesarean Delivery, n.d.). As for you, you'll get dressed in special clothes and be by her side. Take your camera to create memories of your child's first moments!

If the C-section is scheduled for any reason, it won't be before week 39 of the pregnancy. The doctor will give you instructions on how to prepare for the procedure. For example, your partner needs to eat 8 hours before the procedure and drink fluids up to 3 hours prior. You'll arrive at the hospital 2.5 hours before the scheduled time. At the delivery room, she'll receive the same preparation. The surgery takes about an hour. The baby comes out through an incision in your partner's abdomen and uterus after the first 15 minutes, and the rest of the time is for carefully closing the surgical incision (Fink, 2021). Don't worry; neither of you will have to see it since a curtain blocks the sight of the surgery while your partner lies awake. She may feel pressure and some pushing as the doctor guides the baby out, but it won't hurt her. And then, both your partner and the baby spend two more hours recovering, skin-to-skin, getting to know each other, and enjoying their first moments together.

Induction

We've seen what happens during natural vaginal birth and C-sections. Is there another birthing option? Yes, there is. Some-times, doctors opt for a birth induction, which is a way to induce vaginal birth by supplying medications to your partner. First, a little pill is inserted into her vagina near the cervix. Then, the baby gets monitored for a couple of hours to make sure they are perfectly fine. If there are no changes in the cervix after a while, you two may be sent home to wait. If the cervix dilates, the doctor may proceed to break the bag of water, and your partner will be given another medication called Pitocin through an IV to stimu-late contractions (Fink, 2021). Labor will progress from then on, and if everything goes according to plan, she'll deliver the baby as in any other vaginal birth.

After Birth

The first time you see your baby, you may be amazed by their appearance. Their blue or mottled skin is covered in amniotic fluid, the cheesy vernix, and blood. Don't worry! It's all normal, and they'll become rosy pink as they take their first breaths. Your partner will feel immediate relief after the baby comes out, but she's not done yet. Some minutes after giving birth, she'll deliver the placenta, which looks like a huge piece of meat. It won't hurt her! Then, it's the time to cut the umbilical cord—and you may be offered to do so! Snip-snap and... there! Your baby is an independent person.

Shortly after birth, your baby will be dried and warmed, all within your sight, and given to you and your partner as soon as possible. If your partner had a C-section, your baby will be placed in her arms, or skin-to-skin, as you move together as a family to recovery. Most newborns naturally attempt breastfeeding during their first minutes of life. Your partner won't have milk yet, but colostrum, a rich substance that protects the baby with only some drops.

What will doctors do to your newborn? Besides weighing and measuring them, they give them a shot of vitamin K (because it is deficient in some babies) and measure their Apgar scores, which is an observation made 1 minute and 5 minutes after birth to see how well the baby is adapting to life outside the uterus. Apgar scores evaluate the baby's heart rate, breathing, color, muscle tone, and reflexes.

After you are all moved to the hospital room, your baby will spend most of their first 24 hours sleeping as they recover from birth. However, they'll also pee and poo! The first deposition is called meconium. It is dark and sticky and quite difficult to wipe! Most hospitals keep the mother and newborn together all the time, although you can ask a nurse to take the baby away for a short time to sleep or for the new mom to shower.

During the first week after birth—sometimes before getting discharged from the hospital—babies undergo a series of tests called newborn screening, which is required in all U.S. states for at least 21 disorders and in most states for additional ones (de Bellefonds, 2022). Doctors perform blood, hearing, and heart tests on your baby. These tests are meant to detect rare but potentially serious health conditions (such as metabolism or endocrinal disorders) that can be treated if detected early. These tests are perfectly safe for your baby, and most of them are at least partially covered by your health insurance, so make sure to check.

What about your partner? She needs to recover after delivery or C-section. She'll experience a variety of symptoms both if she had a vaginal birth or a C-section, and she may need to take care of her stitching, keeping either her perineum or her incision clean and disinfected. Even if she had a natural birth, she may need stitches if she had an episiotomy or experienced some tearing. During the first few days, she will go through:

- red, heavy bleeding from her vagina (called lochia)
- after-birth pains, as the uterus contracts back to its normal size
- sore nipples or breast tenderness, as she'll spend several hours a day breastfeeding
- exhaustion

- a roller coaster of emotions due to her lack of sleep, hormonal rush, and mixed feelings about becoming a first-time mom (like yourself, she's excited and grateful but also scared!)

WHAT YOU CAN DO

Giving birth is a lot for any woman! Luckily, she'll have your support to go through these first weeks of adjustment. You'll learn to be a family together.

Support Your Partner

Knowing what your partner and baby will likely go through should help ease some of your stress. After all, your primary role in the delivery room is supporting your partner, not adding up to her anxiety! Besides, you need to take care of your mental health to stay in your best version for the sake of your new family. What can you do?

- If possible, visit the delivery room during your hospital tour. "While there's very little you'll be able to change, creating a baseline comfort level can lower stress and anxiety on the day of delivery" (Dashiell, 2022).
- Pack lots of light entertainment to make the long hours of waiting go faster. Reassure your partner she's doing great and that it's normal for labor to take that long.
- During labor, take care of yourself. Your partner can't eat or drink, but you should stay strong and hydrated. Make sure you know where the vending machines are. Try to rest, but don't fall asleep: Your partner will never forgive you! "If your partner isn't sleeping, neither are you. That's just the way it goes. You stayed up 48 hours straight in

college, right? You can do it again now" (The Bump, 2018).

- Turn off your cell phone when your partner is in active labor. Work calls or talking to your parents to share the news can wait!
- Watch your mouth! I know you are tired after long hours standing or massaging your partner's lower back, but complaining about any ache when she is in excruciating pain will not be well-received. Neither will your jokes or comments on how gross something is. To stay safe, only say words if they are supportive.
- Advocate for your partner. She may need your help standing for the birth plan you discussed together, or she may change her mind. In any case, make sure you support her and communicate her wishes to the doctor.
- If you are going to record the birth, discuss with your partner which angles she is okay with! While she may want to share the memories of the event with the rest of the family, she won't feel comfortable with her parents or yours seeing her crotch.

After your baby is born, your partner needs all her energy to recover her strength and breastfeed. She shouldn't do anything other than that. It's your time to get hands-on with your baby!

- Cuddle your baby, hold them, and settle them whenever your partner isn't feeding them so she'll have the chance to rest.
- Change their diapers and bathe them.
- Provide practical and emotional support to your partner. Do the housework, give her a glass of water when she's breastfeeding, and keep telling her what an amazing job she's doing.

- Remind your partner it's okay to need extra help. If things aren't going smoothly, you can talk to her doula or midwife or see a lactation consultant.

Make the Calls

Sometimes, labor doesn't turn out as expected. I don't want to scare you. Chances are everything will be okay, and even if there are complications, they can be promptly addressed and treated. You should know what kind of problems can occur, especially if it's a high-risk pregnancy, the due date is past more than two weeks, or your partner is older. In these scenarios, you may need to decide and ensure both your partner's and baby's safety and well-being.

- Labor may fail to progress when your partner's cervix doesn't dilate, the effacement is slow, the baby is too big, or she's giving birth to more than one baby. Sometimes, you only need to wait a bit longer and reassure your partner to help her relax. However, if complications happen during the active phase, doctors may opt for an intervention. The opposite complication is rapid labor, when contractions are so effective that labor happens faster than usual.
- Monitors may display signs of fetal distress, such as low levels of amniotic fluid, an irregular heartbeat, or problems with muscle tone. It means the baby doesn't appear to be doing well. In some cases, doctors need to get them out by C-section delivery to ensure the baby's status.
- Labor interventions may be needed if the baby is misplaced, such as shoulder dystocia, facing upward, or lying sideways. Doctors may need to use the forceps, manually change the baby's position, or perform a C-section.

- After birth, the baby may need oxygen or medication if they tested low on Apgar scores.
- Every woman loses blood during childbirth, but excessive bleeding can occur when uterine contractions aren't strong enough to compress the blood vessels where the placenta attached to the uterus. This is more common in certain pregnancy conditions, such as multiple births, placenta previa, uterine rupture, prolonged labor, hypertension, obesity, or blood-clogging disorders. Medical treatment—which can go through medication and massages to surgery—is required immediately because the bleeding can be life-threatening.

Going through medical checkups and having access to appropriate health care can prevent or resolve most of these complications. During pregnancy and delivery, always listen to your partner's health provider's advice and trust them. Things may not always go according to the birth plan, but you must reassure your partner it's all for the best.

This is what happened to my friends Daniel and Juliet. Doctors found out at the hospital the baby's head was unable to fit through Juliet's pelvis, something known as cephalopelvic disproportion (CPD). So, they went through a C-section, although it wasn't in the plan. Everything went great, and later that day, Juliet delivered a healthy baby girl.

KEY TAKEAWAYS

We've seen what to expect during different scenarios of giving birth and discussed your role before, during, and after delivery. The following chapter will be about embracing your role as a new dad.

WELCOME TO FATHERHOOD

After spending an extra day at the hospital recovering from her C-section, Juliet and baby girl Amanda were finally discharged. Daniel drove them home, Amanda safely secured in the properly installed car seat, and they finally arrived at their place, where the three of them continued to bond with one another.

Juliet was exhausted, and her incision felt sore. Daniel was permanently attending to both her and the baby, and it didn't help him that the phone kept ringing. People were dying to see little Amanda! To let his partner rest, Daniel had to turn into a sort of goalkeeper with the visitors. Some of them came eager to help, and they were welcomed. They were the ones who volunteered to clean or bring homemade dinners. Some others wanted to be offered a cup of tea and do chit-chat, and they were politely sent away!

During your baby's first three months, your life will be turned upside down—and more than once! This chapter will tell you what you should be aware of and what you should do to support your partner and spend time with your newborn.

WHAT HAPPENS IN...

If you thought pregnancy's week-by-week changes were breathtaking, wait until you see your baby growing and changing day by day! This is an overview of what you can expect.

The First Month

By the time you arrive home, your baby is a tiny little being who weighs less than when they were born. This drop in weight is normal and reverts around their fifth day. Your baby's pediatrician will monitor them closely to see if they start gaining weight according to what's expected, together with their newborn reflexes, which show everything is right on track, and how their umbilical cord is healing. Doctors will also provide reassurance if you are concerned about your newborn's unusual appearance. Their body is all curled up because they are used to being squeezed into the uterus, and their sex organs may be swollen because they are still holding some of your partner's hormones. You may notice certain features, such as a flattened nose or a cone head, which are due to being pulled through the birth canal.

Your baby's needs by this time are simple. Most of the time, they are either eating or sleeping! Their vision is still blurry, but they can see your face when you hold them closely. They already recognize your voice and their mom's scent. Besides supporting your partner with frequent and long sessions of breastfeeding, you are in charge of changing diapers (expect frequent poops at this stage!) and cuddling your newborn a lot.

Newborn babies sleep most of the time and can't tell apart days and nights yet. On average, babies spend around 16.5 hours asleep during their first month, but between 14 and 19 or even 20 hours is normal, too (Felton, 2021). Don't expect all this snoozing to happen at once, though. Babies sleep in short chunks, and they frequently wake to feed. They can breastfeed 8 to 12 times a day, while those who are bottle-fed can go a little longer without needing a bottle. Remind your partner to forget about the clock when it comes to feeding, as it's advisable to do it on demand to regulate milk production.

Other than feeding or sleeping, your newborn will spend plenty of time—yup—crying. It's the only means they have to express their needs! Your newborn cries because they are hungry, tired, over-stimulated, cold, hot, or uncomfortable. At first, you won't be able to tell what they need, but spending a lot of time with your baby and always responding to their crying will make it easier as weeks go by. Don't worry! You can't spoil them by giving them extra affection.

The Second Month

As weeks pass, your newborn begins stretching the times they spend awake—although they still need plenty of sleep. Whenever they are fed, clean, and comfortable, try to stimulate their senses by looking them in the eyes, singing to them, talking to them, and showing them high-contrast pictures in books and vibrant, colorful toys. A baby gym is also a great entertainment place. However, once your little one gets fussy, take them away from all the stimulation and make sure they get a good nap.

At this age, your baby will have some delightfully cute milestones. They start babbling, and at around 6 weeks, their first social smile appears (we call it "social" because younger babies sometimes smile, but only as a reflex of comfort). On the other hand, babies usually cry more, and their fussiness peaks around weeks 6 to 8. Don't worry! They will settle in about a month. In the meantime, keep calm and remember your bond with your baby is already strong enough for you to provide comfort and reassurance when they are at their crankiest.

Other milestones of the second month are discovering their hands and fingers (and taking them to their mouth) and sometimes attempting to roll. To encourage movement, make sure your little one spends 10 to 15 minutes a day in tummy time. They still feed pretty often and keep gaining weight fast, but you may notice their poopy diapers aren't as frequent. During their monthly check-up, their pediatrician will ensure appropriate growth and development.

The Third Month

Your baby is no longer a newborn by now! They control their movements better, turn their head whenever a sound calls their attention, and smile when they see your face. They have new facial expressions and cry in different ways whether they are hungry, sleepy, or scared. Although they won't speak for a long time, their babbling is more developed, and sometimes they can have "conver-sations" with you! During this month, your baby may delight you with their first giggles and laughter.

Babies gain better control of their heads and can lift themselves over their shoulders when lying on their tummy. They also control their hands to grab their favorite toys and sometimes clap them together. Make sure you give them plenty of time to move freely to develop these milestones.

At this age, babies still need to be fed on demand, but they can usually go longer stretches without the breast or bottle. Finding other ways to settle them is important, either by hugging them, singing to them, or whispering. Luckily, if you've followed a consistent bedtime routine, they are already differentiating days and nights and spend more time sleeping when it's dark (yay!). At this age, they are mature enough to start putting them on a schedule. However, this shouldn't be a rigid minute-to-minute plan but a routine that works for everyone around a few anchor moments during the day, such as taking the baby for a walk in their stroller or giving them a nice, relaxing bath before bedtime (Masters, 2023b).

How's Your Partner Doing?

The first 6 weeks after giving birth are the most difficult for your partner. Other than being super busy feeding the baby, she needs to give herself time to fully recover from labor, particularly if she went through a C-section. She will deal with a lot of typical but uncomfortable postpartum symptoms, such as bleeding, hemorrhoids, soreness from the stitches, constipation, backache, and sore nipples... you name it, you get it! At first, she won't recognize her own body, and she may feel emotional all the time.

And since we are discussing emotions, most women experience baby blues during the first weeks, which are feelings of sadness that usually go away after a couple of weeks. However, if you notice your partner gets sadder, more anxious, stressed, and overwhelmed, or expresses she can't take care of the baby or herself and those emotions last longer than a few weeks, you need to talk to her and her doctor—or your baby's doctor as well. These could be symptoms of postpartum depression (PPD), a common condition in women who had babies that needs immediate medical treatment. Sleep deprivation is one of the risk factors for PPD. Remind your partner to get as much sleep as possible, even in catnaps during the day.

WHAT YOU SHOULD KNOW

Let's see how you can stay prepared for these first months of being a dad, what you need to know about bringing home your little bundle of joy, and how often the baby needs to be checked up.

Checklist to Bring Baby Home and Tools Needed

- **Appropriate clothes:** How many outfits does your newborn need? On the one hand, they'll grow into a new size before you know it; on the other hand, they will likely need several changes daily! Keep around a dozen short-sleeved and long-sleeved onesies, nightgowns, socks or booties, one-piece sleepers, possibly a snowsuit if your baby is born in cold weather, and a few fancier outfits for when visitors show up. Just make sure you don't overdress your baby! Dress your newborn as you'd dress yourself. In other words, if it's a warm spring day, you shouldn't put them that knitted vest and matching hat and socks.
- **Newborn check-up schedule:** Before leaving the hospital, check with your health provider about when the baby is due for their first check-up. Ask your baby's doctor, partner's lactation consultant, or a nurse before they discharge them.
- **Approved car seat:** Remember to have the car seat properly installed, if possible under professional supervision, as most car seats in the United States are not installed correctly (Ben-Joseph, 2018). It's the law to sit your baby in an age-appropriate car seat in the back of

your car. Hospitals won't let you go with the baby unless you do! Babies should always ride cars facing backward because, in case of a crash, it's the safest position— although, yes, it may bring some tears as your baby grows up and doesn't get to see you or your partner!

- **Cradle or crib:** Although babies should share the room with their parents, they should sleep on an independent surface. Make sure your baby's mattress is flat and firm, and leave all those fluffy animals, bumpers, and covers out of their crib. You need several baby blankets, but make sure they never cover their face.
- **Feeding supplies:** Get several bottles, nipples, and formula (always check the expiration date). If your partner breastfeeds, just some nursing bras and a nursing pillow will do, although a breast pump and bags to stock milk in the freezer are also advisable.
- **Diaper supplies:** Diapers come in different sizes according to how much your baby weighs. During the first months, they could grow one or two sizes! While it's advisable to buy a diaper supply ahead of time, keep them in more than one size. You also need to stock on baby wipes and ointment.
- **Bathing supplies:** There's no need to rush into giving your baby their first bath, nor do they need to take one every day unless they enjoy it. Get a plastic infant tub that lets you carefully place the baby in a comfortable position— never leave them unsupervised in the bathtub, not for a second! You should also grab some hooded towels and baby shampoo, lotion, and soap to get your little one clean and protect their delicate skin.
- **Medical care:** Before buying any medical supplies, it's best to check with your baby's doctor. However, you will probably need a bulb syringe to help your baby get rid of

mucus, nail clippers so they don't accidentally scratch themselves, anti-gas drops and acetaminophen in case they have a fever, and a thermometer.

How Much to Feed

During the first months of your baby's life, they must be fed on demand, meaning that instead of following a strict schedule, they should be given breastmilk or formula whenever they are hungry. So, let's try another question: How can you tell if your newborn is hungry? You need to learn to read their cues. Sure, if your baby is crying, they are possibly demanding to be fed, but by this point, they are starving and, therefore, are hard to settle. Earlier hunger cues include the baby licking their lips, sticking their tongue out, putting their hand to mouth, opening their mouth, puckering their lips, or rooting (moving their head or jaw searching for the breast).

How often should you feed a newborn? As a rule of thumb, the younger the infant, the more frequently they eat. This is because their tiny stomachs can't hold as much milk at once, and they need frequent refills. During their first month, babies eat between 8 and 12 times a day, and as they grow, so does their intake. "Babies might only take half an ounce per feeding for the first day or two of life, but after that, will usually drink 1 to 2 ounces at each feeding. This amount increases to 2 to 3 ounces by 2 weeks of age" (Jain, 2023). By the time your baby turns 2 months old, they usually take about 4 to 5 ounces every 3 to 4 hours. With breastfeeding, it may be hard to tell exactly how much milk your baby drinks with each intake. However, if they wet 4 to 5 diapers a day and regularly do depositions, that's an indication—together with their weight gain—that they are getting enough food.

According to their weight gain, you can tell if a baby is well fed, overfed, or underfed. Bottle-fed babies have higher chances of being overfed because it's easier for them to drink milk from a bottle. Remember that for babies, suction isn't only about getting food but also about being soothed, and this is where pacifiers are a great help!

At certain points, your baby may seem hungrier than usual. This happens when they go through a growth spurt (a period of rapid growth) and demand more food. These growth spurts usually happen at around 7 to 14 days, between 3 to 6 weeks, at 4 months, and at 6 months (Gavin, 2021). What's important is to keep feeding your baby on demand, even when it means offering them the breast or the bottle more frequently or for longer.

Postpartum Tests and Check-Ups

After bringing your baby home, you'll first get out of the house when you take them to their first check-up, which is due 3 to 5 days after birth. What can you expect from this visit? The health provider will weigh and measure your baby and check their head circumference. This is for monitoring their growth. Then, they'll ask you questions and advise you about feeding, sleeping, peeing and pooping, and overall general behavior. Then, your baby will have a general exam done—the doctor will check their eyes, hips, testicles and circumcision if it's a boy, breathing, and heart rate, review screening tests from the hospital, and update immunizations.

After that first well-baby check-up, you need to bring them again when they are about 2 weeks old, and afterward, when they are 1 month, 2 months, 4 months, and 6 months old unless indicated otherwise. You'll receive a personal child health record (PCHR), which you have to take with you whenever your baby visits their doctor or gets vaccines. You can also fill in information about their milestones and any illnesses, medicines, or accidents.

It's easy to get lost in the mist after having a baby and following up on all of their newborn check-ups, but keep in mind your partner needs medical care, too. Her body went through major trauma by carrying a pregnancy and giving birth, so she must visit her doctor as well. Sadly, 2 out of 5 new moms in the United States miss their postpartum check-ups, which leaves them vulnerable to serious, even life-threatening conditions (March of Dimes, 2023b). So, you should insist your partner gets herself checked no matter how fine she's feeling.

The American College of Obstetricians and Gynecologists (ACOG, 2018) recommends new moms contact their health provider 3 weeks after giving birth, getting ongoing medical care as needed during recovery, and then having a complete medical check-up at week 12 after delivery. Doctors may look for symptoms of post-natal health problems, especially PPD, and give you and your partner advice for contraceptive methods.

WHAT YOU CAN DO

Now that you have an idea of what life after a baby may be like, let's see how to make the most of it.

Support Your Partner

- **Give her water:** Your partner will need lots of fluids and nutritious meals to recover and breastfeed. Whenever she's nursing the baby, give her a glass of water without asking. Make sure she stays hydrated and well-fed. If possible, prepare something she can eat with a single hand!
- **Be the ice provider:** Help her relieve the soreness of her perineal or abdominal incision by handing her fresh ice pads. While she's resting, ask her if she needs anything,

from her phone to the remote control. It will make a difference!

- **Ask for family and friends to help:** Some people are willing to give both of you a hand. Some others just want cute baby pictures to post in their Instagram stories. Filter those visitors and make sure no one overextends their welcome.
- **Let her sleep in the morning:** If she's handling night feedings, try having the baby while you make breakfast and allow her those extra minutes of sleep. It will also give you the chance to spend one-on-one time with your newborn.
- **Treat her:** Now that the baby is born, they receive all the attention, and no one seems to remember the postpartum mom! Surprise her with her favorite flowers, a bar of chocolate, or a sushi take-out she couldn't enjoy for the past nine months.
- **Refrain from making comments about her body:** This means praise, too. She's not feeling herself, and if you compliment her appearance, she may believe you are being condescending or pushing her to get back to your sex life, which is the last thing on her mind right now. It's better to compliment other traits, such as her strength or how great she's doing as a new mom.
- **Watch out for PPD signals:** Talk to her. Most women keep these feelings to themselves because they feel guilty or inadequate, but it's crucial that they receive medical help. "Depression isn't something you should just 'suffer through,' and you definitely shouldn't be ashamed to get the help that you—and your baby—need" (Felton, 2021).
- **Look after your own mental health:** New dads can also suffer from anxiety or depression. In the following chapter, we'll provide tips for self-care for new dads.

Spend Time With Baby

Your partner is the one with the boobs, but soon you'll discover new dads have other baby superpowers! The longer you spend with your newborn, the more ways you'll find to connect with them and establish a strong, loving bond.

- **Hold your baby:** This may seem obvious, but some new dads feel inadequate or fear being too clumsy with their fragile newborn. Practice makes perfect! Be gentle, soft, and warm. Soon, your newborn will recognize you and calm down whenever you hold or cuddle them.
- **Communicate with them:** Just because they can't speak doesn't mean you can't talk to them! Tell them about your day and what you're doing. Describe objects around the house. Smile at them and look them into their eyes. It's never too early to start reading or singing to a baby.
- **Respond to their crying:** Hold your baby gently when they cry, even if you don't know why they are crying. By doing so, you are letting them know they can count on you.
- **Watch for their cues:** When you spend a lot of time with your baby, it becomes easier to understand their needs and respond accordingly. Take a mental note of how they behave when hungry or sleepy. Soon, you'll be able to decipher their cues.
- **Keep them safe:** Learning to wrap your baby is a way of keeping them comfortable and secure.
- **Develop daddy codes:** Singing your own tunes, making silly faces, and being goofy around your baby will soon become part of your unique role as a dad. Your newborn may not respond immediately, but just wait for their first smile and giggles; they will melt your heart.

INTERACTIVE ELEMENT: HOW-TO STEPS

You'll learn to take care of your baby with practice. If it makes you feel more secure, here are a few easy-to-remember, step-by-step instructions on some usual tasks:

Carry and Hold

1. Place one hand under your baby's head for support.
2. Slide the second hand under your baby's bottom.
3. Bend your knees to protect your back.
4. Scoop up the baby, bringing them close to your chest.

Prepare Formula

1. Check the expiration date.
2. Wash your hands.
3. Sterilize bottle and nipples.
4. Add water to the formula if it's concentrated liquid or powder. Do not overdilute.
5. Warm the formula. Test its temperature by putting a few drops on your wrist.
6. Feed the baby. The formula should be used within the hour.
7. Discard what's left in the bottle.

Swaddle

1. Spread the blanket on a firm surface, with one corner pointing up.
2. Fold the top corner down.
3. Place the baby on the swaddle.

4. Take the left side of the blanket and wrap it over your baby's arm and chest.
5. Tuck that side of the blanket underneath their back.
6. Cover your baby's body with the bottom of the blanket.
7. Tuck the right side of the blanket under their left side.
8. Check that the baby is snug, not too loose or too tight.

Burp

1. Hold your baby upright with their head resting on your shoulder.
2. Cup your free hand slightly.
3. Gently pat their back with your cupped hand.

Calm a Crying Baby

1. Always go to your baby whenever they cry.
2. Check their temperature.
3. See if they are hungry or need a new diaper.
4. Hold them close against your body and whisper calm words.
5. Rock them or walk around with them.
6. Sing to them.
7. Offer them a pacifier.
8. If everything fails, sometimes a ride in the stroller or car does wonders.

Put to Sleep

1. Learn to read your baby's tiredness cues.
2. Check that the baby is comfortable.
3. Darken the room and play white noise.
4. Swaddle your baby.

5. Place them in the crib, always on their back, when they are drowsy but still awake.
6. Offer them a pacifier.

KEY TAKEAWAYS

Now you know all the basics about bringing your baby home and what to expect during these first months as a family. Remember: Your baby needs you, but the best you can do for them is look after your partner and give her time to recover. And, speaking about your partner, our last chapter will deal with the two of you, whether you remain a couple or opt to co-parent, as well as some self-care strategies new dads should implement.

IT TAKES TIME

In previous chapters, I told you how my friends Daniel and Juliet started their family. Some decades ago, their family type —two heterosexual, married parents—was considered the norm, but nowadays, this traditional family is just one possibility. In the United States, almost 13 million custodial parents are living with children under age 21, and more than 20% of them are dads, over 2.5 million. "It's slowly becoming more likely for custodial parents to be fathers, especially compared to a few decades ago" (Lazic, 2023).

Single dads aren't something new. Even before divorce was legal, there were always some widowers, right? The novelty is that not only are divorced men actively taking the role of looking after their children, but also, more men are becoming single dads *by choice*. The phenomenon is known as platonic parenting or conscious or elective co-parenting. Sarah Treleaven from *Today's Parent* describes it as "a twist on friends with benefits—the benefits, in this case, being a partner to share in the emotional, physical, psychological, and practical gauntlet of raising a child" (2021).

The favorite way for gay men to become fathers, and currently chosen by 16 million non-married people in the United States (Hope, 2024), co-parenting begins with the active search for a partner, but not in a romantic/sexual way. You look for someone to share the adventure of parenting a child, whether living under the same roof or sharing their custody. Sometimes, their kids are born through fertility treatments; other times, they are adopted. In any case, platonic parenting is becoming a new norm.

In this final chapter, we'll discuss how to integrate being a dad with your relationship with your partner—whether romantic or not—and discover the importance of self-care and how a self-care routine can help you be a better father and partner.

CAN CO-PARENTING WORK?

As mentioned before, conscious co-parenting is the arrangement two or more people make to raise a child without being romantically involved. It requires previous talks about topics related to child-rearing, such as education, religion, parenting styles, views on vaccination, and such. Co-parenting also refers to a friendly divorce in which the couple no longer remains together but keeps interacting and sharing the raising of their child.

People who co-parent need to agree on finances and living arrangements. While in some ways it happens when sharing child custody after a non-conflictive divorce, co-parenting also happens with people who aren't and have never been romantically involved with each other. Therefore, it allows them to focus entirely on the child's needs and well-being. As with any other family model, it has its ups and downs.

The Pros of Co-Parenting

Unlike parallel parenting—when two people split up and divide the custody of their children with little or no interaction with each other—when two people co-parent, they communicate frequently and work together in deciding what's best for their child(ren). Therefore, they provide a unified set of rules and discipline that secures the child by providing them with a stable environment. This is how Keoni Souza, who provides legal counseling to families, puts it: "Whether or not the parents have a romantic relationship with one another is immaterial to their ability to raise healthy and happy kids, so long as their co-parenting relationship is solid" (2019).

If co-parenting happens after a divorce, it helps diffuse tension since the adults put their conflicts aside to focus on making things work for their children. People who opt for platonic co-parenting say it has the best of both worlds. Jessica, a woman from Seattle who co-parents with her best friend from elementary school, says she and Naomi focus on parenting and their friendship, leaving aside the usual conflicts of romantic relationships. "I think it's a lot to match with someone on parental philosophy, willingness to actually share the tasks of parenting, and then add in sexual and romantic chemistry" (Hope, 2024).

Particularly for cis-gender women, the possibility of finding a platonic co-parent relieves the pressure of the "ticking clock," as they no longer feel rushed to find a romantic partner before their age makes it challenging to become pregnant and to carry on a safe pregnancy. Some women decide to take the step by themselves, becoming single moms by choice with the help of a sperm donor. However, sharing the workload of caring for a child usually works best for them.

Platonic parents also share the financial burden of child-rearing, starting from the expensive fertility treatments and moving on with housing arrangements and child education. Sometimes, they manage to live together under the same roof (without sharing the bed); other times, their child spends equal time in both homes.

Some Cons of Co-Parenting

While co-parenting works great for some people, others state it is not for everyone. When it happens after a divorce, you need to set aside your feelings. Every possible resentment or personal conflict with your former spouse must be left behind to co-parent together. This isn't possible when the relationship is particularly conflictive. "If you continue to feel disrespected or unsafe around your ex, this can negatively affect your children as well. The emotional well-being and safety of you and your child must come first" (Dodson, 2024).

As for platonic co-parenting, it may work great, but it takes a lot of planning. And even then, expectations can change after the baby is born. What if one of the co-parents falls in love and wants to start another family? What if one of you gets a job abroad? Besides, sometimes legislation doesn't contemplate these arrangements. For example, if two LGBTQ+ couples decide to co-parent a child, depending on which state the baby is born in, the birth certificate may include only the biological parents.

How to Be a Great Co-Parenting Partner

If you are about to become a dad or have just welcomed your newborn into the world and find yourself co-parenting, you may wonder how to make things work with the other parent(s). Here are some tips for successfully co-parenting a baby:

- **If you are divorced or separated, set your feelings aside:** Consider you are starting a new relationship from scratch with your partner, one focused entirely on the benefit of your child. It's no longer about the two of you; it's about providing stability and happiness to this little person for whom you two are responsible. So, deal with your anger, resentment, or sadness, and don't let them control your actions. Talk about how you feel with a friend, family, or a professional if you need one.
- **Keep the conversations on parenting:** Avoid addressing issues like new relationships or how your ex spends their money. Refrain from making personal remarks. You need to communicate fluently, but only to talk about baby stuff. You don't always need to speak in person, as some matters can be discussed on the phone or by email. However, you must remain open and honest with each other on issues such as medical needs or education.
- **Come up with a plan:** Don't leave anything to chance. Each parent has rights and responsibilities, such as visitation schedules and baby-related expenses. Put them in a contract and stick to them. This will give you clear guidelines and strengthen the co-parenting relationship.
- **Be consistent:** Babies rely on routines. When you decide on your co-parenting schedule, consider that your baby needs frequent visits and quality time with both parents to bond. "Ensure to visit the baby several times a week. When visiting, you must use the time to bond with the infant to familiarize them with your presence. You can feed, soothe, or bathe the newborn if you want" (*Co-Parenting a Newborn*, n.d.). At the same time, consider that your arrangements don't interfere with your baby's feeding and resting times.

- **Consider taking your vacation together:** According to experts, babies and toddlers shouldn't spend too many days apart from either of their parents during their first two years (*Co-Parenting a Newborn*, 2020). While having the baby over for a long weekend is okay, if you want to take them to meet your parents in another state, it would be best to ask your partner if they agree to join you.
- **Revisit rules and expectations:** The agreement you have today may not work in the future. Those visitation schedules that work so great now may need to be redesigned as your baby enters new milestones, such as sleeping fewer naps or beginning kindergarten. Other possible changes are financial challenges (for example, if either of you suddenly lost your job) or meeting a new romantic partner.
- **Be flexible:** People grow and change, and so do families: "Just like in any other family dynamic, your co-parenting relationship and family needs will evolve during your journey, so flexibility and keeping an open mind are key" (Zielger, 2022). Allow yourself and your co-parent that room to grow.

IS SELF-CARE IMPORTANT?

Being a dad will change your life in unimagined ways. It will certainly transform your relationship with your partner, and the relationship with your child will become one of the most meaningful in your existence. However, when I became a dad, I never imagined how deeply it would impact another relationship: That is, the one I have with myself. Looking at my newborn, I understood she needed me at my best and would need me for many years to come. After becoming a father, I stopped smoking and took exercise as a regular habit. I started eating healthier, and I went through a lot of work to heal past trauma so I could be the strong, supportive father she deserved without losing my energy fighting my demons.

Don't Suffer in Silence

Looking after your health is important, and that includes your mental health. Did you know that more than 6 million men in the United States suffer from depression? They become tired, irritable, lose interest in work, and feel worthless. This condition affects dads specifically: 1 in 10 fathers experience PPD or anxiety, and sadly, they are less likely to receive a mental health diagnosis—and, therefore, the treatment they need—than their female partners (Fleming, 2023). New responsibilities, together with the cultural imperative to keep your problems to yourself, put men under a lot of pressure.

This mandate to "man up" only perpetuates the bias of weakness whenever a man expresses discomfort or pain. "The problem is that if men can't speak about their pain, they won't have a way to begin to process and deal with it or reach out for help. With dads, it not only impacts his own life but also his children's lives," explains LaKeisha Fleming from Verywell Mind. It's clear: You are a role model to your children. They do as they see. If you struggle with a mental health issue and they see you actively addressing it, reaching out for help, and openly talking about it with your partner or other loved ones, they'll learn to cope. However, if you hide your pain and mask it with anger, violence, or substance abuse, that's what you'll be teaching them to do in the future.

Self-Care for Dads

A lot has been said about the importance of self-care for new moms, and it's always important to underline it. In previous chapters, we've mentioned several ways in which you should support your partner during pregnancy and after giving birth. However, the only way new dads can fulfill their many new roles is by first caring for themselves. You know the old saying: You can't pour from an empty cup. You need a healthy body, mind, and happiness in your life!

The good news is that, with a little imagination, it is possible to combine self-care activities with being a father. Your child is a huge motivator for embracing new, healthy habits and creating a new routine. Here are some ideas; you'll come up with yours as well!

- **Get a check-up:** You're probably used to driving your partner and your newborn baby back and forth to the doctor's office. Why not do it for you this time?
- **Sign up for a baby and me yoga class:** Although most are labeled "mommy and me," many yoga instructors will happily accept dads in their classes! It's a fantastic way to breathe out your worries, connect with your baby, and gain flexibility at the same time.
- **Personal grooming:** Make shaving a ritual. Invest in a good lotion and moisturizer. Taking care of the skin isn't just for the ladies, you know.
- **Eat healthy:** Since you are doing most of the cooking, seize the opportunity to include more fruits, vegetables, whole grains, and a variety of healthy foods in your diet. Ordering a pizza once a week won't kill you, but a homemade casserole tastes way better!

- **Build a dad community:** Having solid friendships is important for your mental health. While it's natural for some friends to distance themselves after you become a dad, having a child also creates new opportunities for you to make new friends. Go talk to other dads by the swings or organize a barbecue with the families from daycare.
- **Make time for your hobbies:** You won't spend much time building a scale model once your baby is a newborn. Still, as their sleep schedule becomes slightly less erratic, save some time for doing the things you like.
- **Get enough sleep:** This is easier said than done. But one thing is getting out of bed to change your baby so your partner can get some shut-eye, and another is spending those precious hours you could be in bed scrolling down your phone. Practice good sleep hygiene habits and get as much rest as possible.
- **Spend time outdoors:** Being surrounded by nature does wonders for your mental health! Taking your baby in the stroller for a walk is a perfect way to get some exercise, fresh air, and quality time together.
- **Cut down on social media and turn on the music:** Did you know that screen time is bad for your baby? Then, why would it be good for yourself? On the other hand, music significantly improves your well-being and lowers your heart rate and blood pressure (Dolan, 2023).
- **Find professional help:** Finally, if you feel it's too much to take on, never hesitate to reach out to a therapist. It doesn't make you any less of a man, and it will turn you into a better dad.

MAKING TIME FOR YOUR RELATIONSHIPS.

When baby Amanda was 6 months old, Daniel and Juliet finally went on a date. As they toasted with a mocktail, they looked at each other. They barely recognized the person in front of them! Having a baby changes the relationship's dynamics in so many ways! Some are obvious (you knew your partner wouldn't be in the mood for love-making after delivering a 6-pound baby!), and others come totally unexpected.

Couples who have a baby often find themselves constantly arguing. Sleep deprivation, stress, and constant demands from the newborn mean you have less patience than ever and that you don't put your relationship first anymore. Communication becomes merely practical—instead of texting each other "I love U" or fun memes, you replace them with "Get more formula" or "Ped today 2 p.m." Having a baby doesn't leave room for spontaneity—nor energy for your sex life! Both of you crave for "me" time. And if you add your colliding parenting styles, the unavoidable money issues, and grandparents dropping by unexpectedly, well, there you have it! No wonder why the biggest challenge for new parents is not getting divorced, right?

Look at the bright side, though: You've been through a lot, which means you're now stronger than before! Plus, you can do some things to help you work on the relationship and make time for yourselves even after a baby. Here are some tips:

- **Talk about how you feel:** Share how you're living every experience without necessarily expecting the other person to fix things or to have everything figured out. Simply open up about both the joy and rewards, as well as the pain, the struggles, and the doubts.

- **Share some special time:** Maybe you can't plan date nights or go to concerts. But you can share a cup of coffee after a long night taking shifts with your newborn, watch a short sitcom episode, and laugh together when the baby is finally asleep.
- **Work as a team:** This means equally dividing tasks, being kind to one another, and praising each other for your efforts.
- **Set clear boundaries with your extended families:** If now that you have a baby, your parents or in-laws are constantly dropping by, it's time to have a talk and decide how to manage visits. It may work out for the best! Maybe they are so excited about seeing the new baby that they can babysit instead of waiting to be offered some coffee.
- **Be specific:** Instead of complaining about your partner's attitude, ask for specific changes in their behavior. For example, replace "I'm tired of keeping track of everything!" with "Please, include the baby checkups in your calendar app."
- **Get physical:** Maybe sex is still off the table. But you can reconnect by kissing, cuddling, or giving your partner a back rub. Physical intimacy is the key to a healthy, loving relationship.
- **Expand the meaning of "dates":** Maybe you aren't ready to go out to a restaurant and leave the baby with anyone else. But you can still make some time for each other. For example, you can order take-out and set a nice table at home when the baby is out for the night, or you can drop by and surprise your partner on her lunch break at work with a lovely bouquet.
- **Play games:** Plan a game night with your partner instead of automatically turning on the TV. Board games or video games, what matters is having fun together!

- **Create new family routines:** Taking the baby for a walk in the evening, getting in the car and visiting a farmer's market every other Saturday, or eating lunch in the backyard can become new rituals to bring you closer both as a couple and as a family of three.

Be patient with yourself and kind to your partner. It will take time to adjust and find a "new normal." Even then, you'll still face problems and challenges, but tackling them before they get worse is essential. Remember that you can get professional help if you feel stuck and things start falling apart. But working on your relationship isn't just important for the two of you. Communicating and making time can help you be better parents to your newborn baby.

KEY TAKEAWAYS

We've seen how to be there for your baby even if you aren't involved in a romantic relationship with your co-parenting partner. Remember that self-care and making time for your relationship are equally important for happily fulfilling your new role as a dad.

SHARE YOUR WISDOM, SHAPE A DAD'S JOURNEY

Embrace the Magic of Giving Back

"A little kindness goes a long way."

— *UNKNOWN*

People who lend a hand without expecting anything in return often find greater joy and fulfillment in life. So, let's give it a whirl!

Now, let me ask you this...

Would you lend your support to someone you've never met, even if you didn't receive recognition for it?

Who might this person be? Well, they're a lot like you. Or, at least, like the younger you—curious, a bit nervous, and hungry for knowledge but not quite sure where to find it.

My mission? To make the journey of impending fatherhood a breeze for dads like you. Every word I write stems from this mission. And, the only way for me to fulfill it is by reaching... well... everyone.

And this is where you come into play. It's true what they say—people often judge a book by its cover (and its reviews). So here's my humble plea on behalf of a struggling first-time dad you've yet to meet:

Would you consider leaving a review for this book?

Simply scan the QR code below to leave your review:

Your act of kindness won't cost a penny and requires just a minute of your time, yet it holds the power to transform a fellow dad's life. Your review might just...

Provide invaluable guidance during pregnancy, fostering confidence and strengthening familial bonds.

To Leave A Review Go To:
https://bit.ly/123dad

- Or Scan Below -

SCAN BY CAMERA

CONCLUSION

You've reached the end of the book, but your parenting journey has just begun, and it is meant to last a lifetime. Being a father, especially being as involved as millennial dads are, is always a challenge. Hopefully, you are better prepared to face this lifelong adventure by now! By applying the lessons you learned from this book, be confident you will be a fantastic dad. Anytime you feel in doubt, remember the CRAFT method: Consider, Recognize, Awareness, Fatherhood, and Time. Think of it as a guideline as you enter fatherhood.

I hope you'll find some of the tips and suggestions provided helpful. There's no single answer to how to be a dad, as it's different for each one. You'll come up with your own unique way. However, having a guide to help you through pregnancy and beyond will help ease your doubts and gain confidence in your parenting skills. I promise: It gets easier in time.

Thank you for letting me walk you through this journey. One final request: If you enjoyed the book, kindly leave a review to help me reach out to new dads-to-be.

Happy parenting!

GLOSSARY

Amniotic sac: The bag of water that protects the baby inside the uterus.

Apgar: A quick test performed on the baby during the first minutes after birth.

Baby blues: Mood swings experienced by most women in the first weeks after giving birth.

Blastocyst: The cluster of cells that will eventually develop into an embryo.

Braxton-Hicks: These are "training" contractions that a pregnant woman can feel throughout the second half of the pregnancy. Unlike real contractions, they are irregular and fade when the woman changes her position or rests.

Colostrum: The first form of milk produced by the woman's breasts immediately after giving birth. It is the newborn's first food.

Fertility cliff: A theoretical point in a lifetime when the ability to get pregnant decreases.

Fertility window: The five days before ovulation and the day of ovulation are the moments when a couple can conceive a baby.

HCG: Human chorionic gonadotropin is a pregnancy-induced hormone that can be tracked in blood or a home urine pregnancy test.

Lanugo: A soft layer of hair the fetus grows during the second trimester, which covers their entire skin and keeps them protected.

Lochia: Heavy vaginal bleeding that happens after giving birth.

Meconium: The baby's first deposition after birth.

Ovulation: The process in which a woman's ovary releases an egg. It usually happens once a month, around 2 weeks before a woman's period.

PPD: Postpartum depression. It's a frequent condition a woman can experience after giving birth when baby blues doesn't naturally get better. It requires medical treatment.

Preeclampsia: A common pregnancy-induced disease usually noticeable by high blood pressure.

Zygote: The unique, single-cell product of fecundation of a sperm and an egg.

BIBLIOGRAPHY

After your baby is born: for partners of birthing mothers. (n.d.). Raising Children Network. https://raisingchildren.net.au/pregnancy/pregnancy-for-partners/early-parenting/after-your-baby-is-born-for-partners

The American College of Obstetricians and Gynecologists. (2018, May). *Optimizing postpartum care.* https://www.acog.org/clinical/clinical-guidance/committee-opinion/articles/2018/05/optimizing-postpartum-care

Antenatal classes - preparing you for the birth. (n.d.). Tommy's. https://www.tommys.org/pregnancy-information/im-pregnant/antenatal-care/antenatal-classes-preparing-you-birth

Antenatal classes. (2023, May). Pregnancy, Birth, & Baby. https://www.pregnancybirthbaby.org.au/antenatal-classes

Antenatal classes. (2024, January 17). NHS. https://www.nhs.uk/pregnancy/labour-and-birth/preparing-for-the-birth/antenatal-classes/

Are you pregnant? Here are the early signs and symptoms of pregnancy. (2021). Health Partners. https://www.healthpartners.com/blog/first-symptoms-of-pregnancy/

Ayuda, T. (2021, August 17). *What to expect from third-trimester prenatal appointments.* Babycenter. https://www.babycenter.com/pregnancy/health-and-safety/third-trimester-prenatal-visits_9346

Batcha, B. & Srinivasan, H. (2023, January 5). *A nine-month plan for getting your family's finances in order pre-baby.* Parents. https://www.parents.com/pregnancy/considering-baby/financing-family/a-nine-month-plan-for-getting-your-familys-finances-in-order-pre-baby/

Baby's first 24 hours. (2022, September). Pregnancy, Birth & Baby. https://www.pregnancybirthbaby.org.au/babys-first-24-hours

Bean, S. (2019). *Parenting responsibilities: 10 things you are (and aren't) responsible for as a parent.* Empowering Parents. https://www.empoweringparents.com/article/parenting-responsibilities-10-things-you-are-and-arent-responsible-for-as-a-parent/

Ben-Joseph, E.P. (2018, June). *Bringing your baby home.* Kids Health. https://kidshealth.org/en/parents/bringing-baby-home.html

Ben-Joseph, E.P. (2022, July). *Your child's checkup: 3 to 5 days.* Kids Health. https://kidshealth.org/en/parents/checkup-2weeks.html

Bogle, J. (2021, August 10). *11 ways dads can practice self-care and why they should (yes, even you!).* The Dad. https://www.thedad.com/dads-self-care/

Bonding and attachment: newborns. (2018). Raising Children Network. https://rais ingchildren.net.au/newborns/connecting-communicating/bonding/bonding-newborns

Brewster, A. (2023, July 5). *How to support your partner after birth.* Today's Parent. https://www.todaysparent.com/baby/postpartum-care/how-to-support-your-wife-after-birth/

The Bump. (2018, February 28). *He said WHAT in the delivery room? Tips for dads on delivery day.* https://www.thebump.com/a/he-said-what-in-the-delivery-room

Can I get pregnant just after my period has finished? (2021, July 8). NHS. https://www. nhs.uk/common-health-questions/pregnancy/can-i-get-pregnant-just-after-my-period-has-finished/

Case, H. (n.d.). *7 things you need when bringing Baby home.* Kinsa Health. https:// home.kinsahealth.com/post/7-things-you-need-when-bringing-baby-home

Choosing the right healthcare provider for pregnancy and childbirth. (2022). MedLine Plus. https://medlineplus.gov/ency/patientinstructions/000596.htm

Cleveland Clinic. (2022a, November 28). *Pregnancy tests.* https://my.clevelandclinic. org/health/diagnostics/9703-pregnancy-tests

Cleveland Clinic. (2022b, November 14). *Pregnancy complications.* https://my.cleve landclinic.org/health/articles/24442-pregnancy-complications

Cleveland Clinic. (2023). *Fetal development.* https://my.clevelandclinic.org/health/ articles/7247-fetal-development-stages-of-growth

Common tests during pregnancy. (n.d.). John Hopkins Medicine. https://www.hopkins medicine.org/health/wellness-and-prevention/common-tests-during-preg nancy

Co-parenting a newborn. (n.d.). 2 Houses. https://www.2houses.com/en/blog/co-parenting-a-newborn-how-to-do-it-successfully

Co-parenting a newborn. (2020, October 8). Talking Parents. https://talkingparents. com/parenting-resources/coparenting-a-newborn

Cross, C.I. (2022). *Why can't I get pregnant?* John Hopkins Medicine. https://www. hopkinsmedicine.org/health/conditions-and-diseases/why-cant-i-get-pregnant

Dad-to-be guide: 10 facts for the third trimester. (2019). NCT. https://www.nct.org.uk/ pregnancy/dads-be/dad-be-guide-10-facts-for-third-trimester

Dashiell, C. (2022, April 8). *4 essential tips for men who are new to the delivery room.* Fatherly. https://www.fatherly.com/parenting/dads-delivery-room-stress

de Bellefonds, C. (2022, February 14). *Newborn screenings: What tests will my baby get in the hospital?* What to Expect. https://www.whattoexpect.com/first-year/ health-and-safety/newborn-screening-tests-and-procedures/

Deibel, P.T. (2020, March 23). *Pregnant? Here are 4 things to think about when choosing a doctor or midwife.* UNC Health Talk. https://healthtalk.unchealthcare.org/preg nant-here-are-4-things-to-think-about-when-choosing-a-doctor-or-midwife/

Dodson, J. (2024, February 20). *What is co-parenting? The pros and cons to consider.* Better Help. https://www.betterhelp.com/advice/parenting/what-is-co-parenting-the-pros-and-cons-to-consider/

Dolan, M. (2023, June 5). *The 8 best things dads can do for themselves in honor of Father's Day.* Everyday Health. https://www.everydayhealth.com/healthy-living/best-things-dads-can-do-for-themselves-in-honor-of-fathers-day/

Donaldson-Evans, C. (2023a, October 5). *1 & 2 weeks pregnant.* What to Expect. https://www.whattoexpect.com/pregnancy/week-by-week/weeks-1-and-2.aspx

Donaldson-Evans, C. (2023b, October 5). *17 weeks pregnant.* What to Expect. https://www.whattoexpect.com/pregnancy/week-by-week/week-17.aspx

Donaldson-Evans, C. (2023c, October 5). *40 weeks pregnant.* What to Expect. ?

Donaldson-Evans, C. (2021, August 6). *Signs of labor.* What to Expect. https://www.whattoexpect.com/pregnancy/labor-signs

Donovan Mauer, E. (2017, May 17). *What happens at the hospital when you deliver?* The Bump. https://www.thebump.com/a/what-to-expect-at-the-hospital-during-labor

Felton, K. (2021, October 25). *Baby month 1: Your newborn guide.* What to Expect. https://www.whattoexpect.com/first-year/month-1

Fink, J. (2021, August 14). *Labor and delivery: What to expect at the hospital.* Healthgrades. https://www.healthgrades.com/right-care/pregnancy/labor-and-delivery-what-to-expect-at-the-hospital

First trimester: Tips for dads to be. (2019). NCT. https://www.nct.org.uk/pregnancy/dads-be/first-trimester-tips-for-dads-be

Five factors to consider whether you are ready for a baby. (n.d.) IFEC. https://www.ifec.org.hk/web/en/other-resources/hot-topics/5-factors-to-consider-whether-you-are-ready-for-a-baby.page

Fleming, L. (2023, June 13). *We can't ignore our dads' mental health, even if they try to.* Verywell Mind. https://www.verywellmind.com/dads-mental-health-matters-5409299

Foods to avoid when pregnant. (2019). Pregnancy Birth & Baby. https://www.pregnancybirthbaby.org.au/foods-to-avoid-when-pregnant

From newborn to 15 months old, here's your new baby's checkup schedule. (2021). Health Partners. https://www.healthpartners.com/blog/well-baby-visits-schedule/

Fuentes, A. (2018, August). *Prenatal test: First trimester screening.* Kids Health. https://kidshealth.org/en/parents/prenatal-screen.html

Gavin, M.L. (2021, November). *Formula feeding FAQs: How much and how often.* Kids Health. https://kidshealth.org/en/parents/formulafeed-often.html

Geddes, J. K. (2021, June 14). *How to create a birth plan.* What to Expect. https://www.whattoexpect.com/pregnancy/labor-and-delivery/birth-plan/

Geddes, J.K. (2023, October 25). *Hospital bag checklist.* What to Expect. https://www. whattoexpect.com/pregnancy/checklist/hospital-packing.aspx

Geddes, J.K. (2021, May 10). *Hospital pre-registration for labor and delivery.* What to Expect. https://www.whattoexpect.com/pregnancy/labor-and-delivery/ preparing/hospital-or-birthing-center.aspx

Gize, A., Eyassu, A., Nigatu, B. *et al.* Men's knowledge and involvement on obstetric danger signs, birth preparedness, and complication readiness in Burayu town, Oromia region, Ethiopia. *BMC Pregnancy Childbirth* 19, 515 (2019). https://doi. org/10.1186/s12884-019-2661-4

Gouza, M. (2022, August 10). *Fertility cliff myth: Exploring age, reproductive health, and fertility realities.* Nutrisense. https://www.nutrisense.io/blog/is-the-fertility-cliff-a-myth

Gurevich, R. (2022, November 29). *Why can't I get pregnant? 11 possible reasons.* Very-well Family. https://www.verywellfamily.com/why-cant-i-get-pregnant-if-im-healthy-1959936

Higuera, V. (2020, June 18). *7 things to consider when choosing a pediatrician.* Health-line. https://www.healthline.com/health/childrens-health/how-to-choose-a-pediatrician

Hoffmann, J. (2023, June 6). *The importance of self-care for dads.* Williamsburgh Chiropractic. https://www.williamsburgchirony.com/blog/importance-self-care-dads

Holland, K. (2023, March 10). *17 pregnancy do's and don'ts that may surprise you.* Healthline. https://www.healthline.com/health/pregnancy/dos-and-donts

Holsey Stewart, D. (n.d.). *9 ways to make time for your partner after the baby arrives.* Babycenter. https://www.babycenter.com/family/relationships/9-ways-to-make-time-for-your-partner-after-the-baby-arrives_365

Hope, A. (2024, February 4). *Here's how platonic parenting works.* Parents. https:// www.parents.com/parenting/dynamics/how-platonic-parenting-works/

How to prepare your baby's nursery. (n.d.). SMA Nutrition. https://www.smababy.co. uk/pregnancy/nursery-preparation

Jacobson, J.D. (2022, April 19). *Prenatal care in your third trimester.* Medline Plus. https://medlineplus.gov/ency/patientinstructions/000558.htm

Jain, S. (2023, August 6). *How often and how much should your baby eat?* Healthy Chil-dren. https://www.healthychildren.org/English/ages-stages/baby/feeding-nutri tion/Pages/how-often-and-how-much-should-your-baby-eat.aspx

Johnson, T.C. (2022, August 25). *Choosing a health care provider for your pregnancy and childbirth.* WebMD. https://www.webmd.com/baby/pregnancy-choosing-obstetric-health-care-provider

Johnson, T.C. (2023, March 22). *Second-trimester tests during pregnancy.* WebMD. https://www.webmd.com/baby/second-trimester-tests

Johnson, T.C. (2023, March 22). *First trimester tests during pregnancy.* WebMD. https://www.webmd.com/baby/first-trimester-tests

Kam, K. (2023, June 9). *How often do I need prenatal visits?* WebMD. https://www.webmd.com/baby/how-often-do-i-need-prenatal-visits

Kashtan, P. (2023, May 30). *Your ultimate checklist of baby essentials.* The Bump. https://www.thebump.com/a/checklist-baby-essentials

Kashtan, P. (2024, January 19). *Hospital bag checklist: What to pack in hospital bag.* The Bump. https://www.thebump.com/a/checklist-packing-a-hospital-bag

Kelly, K. (2022, November 17). *10 labor and delivery support tips for partners.* Parents. https://www.parents.com/pregnancy/giving-birth/labor-support/labor-deliv ery-advice-dads/

Kennard, J. (2022, June 25). *A partner's guide to pregnancy in the third trimester.* Verywell Family. https://www.verywellfamily.com/pregnancy-guide-for-men-the-third-trimester-2328988

HealthPartners. (2021). *Labor signs and symptoms: What to expect as labor approaches and begins.* https://www.healthpartners.com/blog/labor-signs-and-symptoms/

LaBracio, J. (2023, December 6). *Ultimate hospital bag checklist for mom and baby.* Babylist. https://www.babylist.com/hello-baby/what-to-pack-in-your-hospital-bag

Lazic, M. (2023, May 20). *30+ divisive child custody statistics.* Legal Jobs. https://legaljobs.io/blog/child-custody-statistics

Livingston, G. & Parker, K. (2019, June 12). *8 facts about American dads.* Pew Research Center. https://www.pewresearch.org/short-reads/2019/06/12/fathers-day-facts/

LoMonaco, J.L. (2022). *How your body and brain change when you become a dad.* Cradlewise. https://cradlewise.com/blog/how-fatherhood-changes-your-body-and-brain

Making a birth plan. (2023, August). Pregnancy, Birth, and Baby. https://www.preg nancybirthbaby.org.au/making-a-birth-plan

March of Dimes. (2020, July). *Newborn screening tests for your baby.* https://www.marchofdimes.org/find-support/topics/parenthood/newborn-screening-tests-your-baby

March of Dimes. (2023a, September). *Your body after baby: The first 6 weeks.* https://www.marchofdimes.org/find-support/topics/postpartum/your-body-after-baby-first-6-weeks

March of Dimes. (2023b, September). *Your postpartum checkups.* https://www.marchofdimes.org/find-support/topics/postpartum/your-postpartum-checkups

Masters, M. (2023a, January 6). *2-month-old baby.* What to Expect. https://www.whattoexpect.com/first-year/month-by-month/month-2.aspx

Masters, M. (2023b, January 19). *3-month-old baby*. What to Expect. https://www. whattoexpect.com/first-year/month-by-month/month-3.aspx

Masters, M. (2021, November 5). *A partner's guide to life after childbirth*. What to Expect. https://www.whattoexpect.com/pregnancy/for-dad/life-after-child birth.aspx

Mauer, E. (2019, December 3). *A look at why relationships change after you have a baby*. Healthline. https://www.healthline.com/health/parenting/relationship-changes-after-baby

Mayo Clinic. (2022, December 23). *Home pregnancy tests: Can you trust the results?* https://www.mayoclinic.org/healthy-lifestyle/getting-pregnant/in-depth/home-pregnancy-tests/art-20047940

Mum's first few days after giving birth. (2021). Pregnancy, Birth, and Baby. https://www.pregnancybirthbaby.org.au/mums-first-few-days-after-giving-birth

Murray, D. (2023, August 16). *How to choose a name for your baby?* Parents. https://www.parents.com/baby-names-4014180

Nash, S.L. (2022, June 20). *9 questions to ask before deciding to have a baby*. Psychcentral. https://psychcentral.com/lib/what-you-need-to-consider-before-having-kids

Nguyen, T.P. (2022, July). *Prenatal tests: First trimester*. Kids Health. https://kidshealth.org/en/parents/tests-first-trimester.html

Nguyen, T.P. (2022, July). *Prenatal tests: Second trimester*. Kids Health. https://kidshealth.org/en/parents/tests-second-trimester.html

Nguyen, T.P. (2022, July). *Prenatal tests: Third trimester*. Kids Health. https://kidshealth.org/en/parents/tests-third-trimester.html

Nuñez, A. (2022, April 19). *How to find the best pediatrician for your baby*. What to Expect. https://www.whattoexpect.com/pregnancy/checklist/potential-baby-doctor.aspx

1-2 months: newborn development. (n.d.). Raising Children. https://raisingchildren. net.au/newborns/development/development-tracker/1-2-months

Parenthood and your relationship. (n.d.). Better Health. https://www.betterhealth.vic. gov.au/health/healthyliving/parenthood-and-your-relationship

Pathak, N. (2021, March 19). *Second trimester tips*. WebMD. https://www.webmd. com/baby/second-trimester-tips

Pregnancy - Signs and symptoms. (2022). Better Health Channel. https://www.better health.vic.gov.au/health/healthyliving/pregnancy-signs-and-symptoms

Preparing your baby's room. (n.d.). Mustela. https://www.mustelausa.com/blogs/mustela-mag/preparing-your-baby-s-room

Risks of complication at every stage of pregnancy (n.d.). Birth Injury Help Center. https://www.birthinjuryhelpcenter.org/complication-pregnant.html

Rockliffe, L. (2023, March 10). *The importance of social support in pregnancy and ways*

to connect with others. Tommy's. https://www.tommys.org/pregnancy-informa
tion/pregnancy-news-blogs/pregnancy-news-blogs-being-pregnant/impor
tance-social-support

Rodgers, L. (2022, June 13). *Week-by-week pregnancy advice for expecting dads and partners.* What to Expect. https://www.whattoexpect.com/pregnancy/for-dad/
week-by-week-pregnancy-advice-dads-partners/

Sample birth plan template. (2022, August). The American College of Obstetricians and Gynecologists. https://www.acog.org/womens-health/health-tools/
sample-birth-plan

Second trimester: 10 big things to think about for dads. (2017, May). NCT. https://www.
nct.org.uk/pregnancy/dads-be/second-trimester-10-big-things-think-about-
for-dads

Sheahan, K.P. (2019, September). *Choosing a pediatrician for your new baby.* Kids health. https://kidshealth.org/en/parents/find-ped.html

Sinrich, J. (2021, May 7). *How to prepare for a baby financially.* What to Expect. https://www.whattoexpect.com/pregnancy/checklist/finances.aspx

6 easy self-care tips for dads. (2023). Didofy. https://didofy.com/parenting-advice/6-
easy-self-care-tips-for-dads

Smith, L. (2018, June 27). *Ten common labor complications.* Medical News Today. https://www.medicalnewstoday.com/articles/307462

Souza, K. (2019). *Is platonic parenting or co-parenting for you?* Keoni Souza Law. https://www.keonisouzalaw.com/post/is-platonic-parenting-or-co-parenting-
for-you

Stein, E., Gordon, S. & Riley, L. (2022, December 19). *9 signs labor is near: How to tell your baby will come soon.* Parents. https://www.parents.com/pregnancy/giving-
birth/signs-of-labor/signs-of-approaching-labor/

Sullivan, D. (2020, April 20). *The importance of checkups in the second trimester.* Healthline. https://www.healthline.com/health/pregnancy/second-trimester-
checkups-tests

Sumner, C. & Scholsberg, S. (2023, January 4). *7 marriage problems after baby and how to solve them.* Parents. https://www.parents.com/parenting/relationships/stay
ing-close/marriage-after-baby/

Terreri, C. (2017, June 5). *To know or not to know your baby's sex - Pros & cons of finding out or keeping it secret.* Lamaze. https://www.lamaze.org/Giving-Birth-
with-Confidence/GBWC-Post/to-know-or-not-to-know-your-babys-sex-
pros-cons-of-finding-out-or-keeping-it-secret

Tete, S. (2024, January 24). *A complete guide on parental rights and responsibilities.* Stylecraze. https://www.stylecraze.com/articles/parental-rights-responsibili
ties/

Treleaven, S. (2021, July 15). *Why more people are having babies with their platonic friends.* Today's Parent. https://www.todaysparent.com/family/parenting/platonic-parenting-having-babies-with-friends/

Understanding your menstrual cycle. (2022, March 6). Tommy's. https://www.tommys.org/pregnancy-information/planning-a-pregnancy/how-to-get-pregnant/understanding-your-menstrual-cycle

Unplanned cesarean delivery. (n.d.). MoBap Baby. https://www.mobapbaby.org/Labor-Delivery/Types-of-Birth/Unplanned-Cesarean

Walsh, K. (2022, June 10). *What to eat in the first trimester.* What to Expect. https://www.whattoexpect.com/pregnancy/eating-well-menu/first-trimester.aspx

What to expect in the delivery room. (n.d.). Blue Kansas City. https://www.bluekc.com/resources/article/pregnancy/what-expect-delivery-room

Your baby's check-ups after they are born. (2021, March 25). Tommy's. https://www.tommys.org/pregnancy-information/after-birth/your-babys-check-ups-after-they-are-born

Your pregnancy week by week. (2018) What to Expect. https://www.whattoexpect.com/pregnancy/week-by-week/

0-1 month: newborn development. (n.d.). Raising Children. https://raisingchildren.net.au/newborns/development/development-tracker/0-1-month

Zielger, A. (2022, April 12). *Tips for successful co-parenting with a platonic friend.* The Bump. https://www.thebump.com/a/platonic-co-parenting-tips